When I Came West

Also by Laurie Wagner Buyer

MEMOIR
Spring's Edge: A Ranch Wife's Chronicles

FICTION
Side Canyons

POETRY AND CHAPBOOKS
Across the High Divide
Red Colt Canyon
Glass-eyed Paint in the Rain
Braintanning Buckskin: A Lesson for Beginners
Blue Heron

When I Came West

Laurie Wagner Buyer

∾

UNIVERSITY OF OKLAHOMA PRESS : NORMAN

Library of Congress Cataloging-in-Publication Data

Buyer, Laurie Wagner, 1954–
When I came West / Laurie Wagner Buyer.
p. cm.
ISBN 978-0-8061-4059-9 (pbk. : alk. paper) 1. Buyer, Laurie
Wagner, 1954– —Homes and haunts—Montana. 2. Women
college students—United States—Biography. 3. Vietnam War,
1961–1975—Veterans—United States—Biography. 4. Wilderness
areas—Montana. 5. Wilderness survival—Montana. 6. Montana—
Description and travel. I. Title.
PS3552.U8944Z46 2009
818'.54—dc22
[B]   2008050121

The paper in this book meets the guidelines for permanence and
durability of the Committee on Production Guidelines for Book
Longevity of the Council on Library Resources, Inc. ∞

1 2 3 4 5 6 7 8 9 10

In memory of Little Fawn

When I Came West

Red Fox

A red fox three-legs her way over the last inches of asphalt. She tips into the ditch, disappears, reappears still gimpy, and limps to the edge of the backyard aspens. Her tongue lolling, she turns to stare at my Jeep stopped in the middle of the street. Her paw-raised posture states "confused and in pain," but her eyes still say "not afraid." Like her, I do not belong in the Rolling Park subdivision in the mountain town of Woodland Park, Colorado. Like her, I am confused and in pain. But unlike the fox, I am afraid—more afraid, perhaps, than I have been since I first turned my nose west thirty years ago and followed the scent of wild places to their source.

Although I spotted fox tracks often enough in Montana, Wyoming, and Colorado to know that the canny creatures shared the same spaces I knew and loved, in that trio of decades I caught only a few glimpses of them zipping across remote roadways. Now, within a handful of weeks, looking out the picture window of my mother's ranch-style home, I have seen foxes a dozen times, sauntering through the trees, trotting

up the driveway, sprinting ahead of neighborhood dogs panting in pursuit. Whether my sightings have been of the hurt-
paw fox or of several different foxes, I cannot tell. I like to think
it is the same animal, one who has come down from a wilderness haunt, sent to serve as a spirit guide to help me find my
way through the unsettling ache of being a town dweller.

A car approaches from behind, and I glance in my rearview
mirror. A herd of t-shirted teenagers crammed into a battered,
souped-up Firebird fling their arms in my direction. The vehicle looks like it is trying to take flight. Taking my foot off the
Jeep's brake, I creep to the side of the street. The Firebird flies
past, gears growling out a young man's disenchantment with a
middle-aged woman who had the audacity to stop and study
a crippled fox. I search the trees. She is still there in the shade,
swiping her injured limb in the air like she is waving. An
expression akin to a smirk crosses her face. She yawns. She
laughs at me, bored beyond belief at my insecurity.

I do not quite comprehend my new uncertainty. How did
I end up here, surrounded by houses, reduced to the fate of
walking concrete sidewalks or macadam trails amid traffic,
joggers, and bicyclists? I am lost and alone. Stately ponderosa
pines grace every spot not covered by buildings and byways.
Miles of national forest radiate out from the deeded land. I am
allowed to hike there if I hop in the Jeep, drive a few miles to a
trailhead, pay a fee, and take care when and where I stop to pee.

Perverse as it sounds, I admit to being spoiled and selfish. At
heart I am unwilling to share my private landscapes with others. Traversing the same trail as someone else feels adulterous.
The sin of my feet kissing soil and rock that I don't know inti-
mately and to which I have no claim is a sensation ripe with
trespass. For too many years, tucked away in wilderness strong-
holds or sequestered on remote ranches, I stepped out cabin
doors and embraced thousands of acres of untrampled country. I consorted with deer, elk, and moose, paid homage to
hawks and ravens. I waited for the owl or killdeer's call, stum-

bled onto fresh bear scat, and searched for trout shadows in streams. I allowed the wind to have her wicked way with me, and honored winter's harsh cold and deep snow because the wrathful weather drove the smattering of tourists and summer-season visitors out of the high country. I paid the price for my nefarious love affair with the land through hard work. I tended to household chores and the care and feeding of domestic animals belonging to the men who allowed me to live with them. Never easy, the romantic, passionate highs naturally dipped down into depressed squabbles. Cabin-fever complaints and furious accusations of one-sided affection became common. Threats meant nothing. The land, the most unyielding of all lovers, simply said, "If you don't like it here, leave."

Until recently, I stayed—sometimes hanging on with the tenacity of fingernails gouged into the cliff's edge. Often I did so against my own better judgment. Frequently I did so against the concerned advice of family and friends, and occasionally in the face of ridiculous odds and unsavory outcomes. I stayed because the land was my life, my inspiration, my sassy muse. The land became my reason for staying alive. Without the land, without the West, who would I be? Where would I call home?

After the years of toughing out a homestead lifestyle on the Northfork of the Flathead River in far northern Montana, I knew I belonged to the West, and the West, in her own intractable, implacable way, belonged to me. It was never a marriage made in heaven. It was always a love affair that hung in delicate balance just above the hellish flames of unhealthy obsession. In those matters of the heart, wherein affection and addiction braid need and want inexplicably together, I often found myself an unwitting bystander. I succumbed, a victim of my body's desire for raw earth beneath my feet and my spirit's restless yearning for unmarred horizons and unfettered wandering. I said once that I came west because I fell in love with a man, but I stayed because I fell in love with the land. It was a true statement when I was twenty, and is truer still as I stare the shifty

gaze of fifty down to the wire. Only now, like the red fox that
was hit by a vehicle, attacked by dogs, or caught in a trap,
I limp my hesitant way into an uncertain future.

I endured earlier short separations from the land with a
braced back and a painted-on smile. Divorce from the land,
banishment from a way of life I hold much too dear, feels
unbearable. The experience remains a kind of pain I struggle
to name or give voice to. Agony sounds affected. Grief seems
almost superficial. Indescribable loss borders on illusion. After
all, how can I lose something that never belonged to me in
the first place? Why did I allow myself to love something so
exquisitely tangible, but in the end inaccessible? A neighboring
rancher once said, "It is plumb foolishness to love something
that can't love you back."

My improbable infatuation with wilderness landscapes
caught me unawares. A child who had never camped out, a
teenager who had never hiked, a college student who had never
seen any animal beyond squirrels and birds in the wild, I harbored no notion whatsoever that the trillion and one diamond
chips of sunlight reflecting off pristine snow would create an
engagement more binding than any carat-sized hunk of crystal
purchased at great price from Tiffany's. Once I touched the
weathered texture of wind-worn wood and water-smoothed
stone, let my lips sip the icy elixir of the river, I was smitten.
When I allowed my unclothed flesh to absorb the caress of
spring sun, the sharp nip of autumn's temperamental breeze,
the teasing twist of summer grass around my calves, I was lost.
I fell in love with the sacredness of dirt and air, all flourishing
things, and abundant animal life. I promised I would do anything to not have to return to the secular world of day jobs,
retirement worries, and stressed-out nights in front of a
television.

Like most young women enmeshed in the first great love
of their lives, I began to write. With no camera, no talent for
painting or drawing, the only means I found available to cap-

ture the face and temperament of my lover was words. Small thumbnail sketches at first, like these lines written my first spring in the West: "Raw winds blow in the dawn, catching the mare on guard, her steamy breath enfolding the one born too soon for spring." I wrote longer poems and stories, most of which I mailed back to Illinois to my mother and father, my sisters, or left-behind friends. After wood and water chores, milking, feeding, cooking, cleaning, whenever I had free time, if my eyes were not focused inside the pages of a book, they were glued to the lines of legal pads. I scribbled. I scratched out a plethora of sentences and phrases in an attempt to find the right words to express the tangle of newfound emotions attached to events that happened daily right outside the door. The river at flood stage. A cow elk barking from the opposite bank. Coyotes calling. The bewitching cry of the loon. The whoosh of a redtail's wings as it made a dive for chickens scratching scattered seed in the sun. The live-in skunk's pervasive odor. Slick birth fluids. Nursing the kid goats that lived, flinging the ones that died onto rooftops for ravens. Cats mewing for morning milk. Spotting a cougar racing from cliff-edge shadow to jack-pine sanctuary. I never found enough time or the proper process to capture everything that bombarded my heart and mind. Still I undertook the challenge.

Trying to understand this unwieldy and intractable passion for a barely known landscape, I turned to the men and women who had dedicated their lives and sacrificed their hearts in similar affairs. My first nonfiction article, titled "A Man Alone," sold to *Western Horseman* in 1978. The acceptance letter from publisher Dick Spencer and the accompanying check for one hundred dollars set my course. While I received countless rejections for my poetry over the next quarter of a century, my nonfiction articles appeared in such magazines as *Farm and Ranch Living, Beef, Horse and Rider, The Fence Post, Cowboy, Roundup,* and *Colorado Country Life.* The avocation fed my need to work with words and filled my pathetic bank account with enough funds to purchase postage stamps. I never thought of myself as a writer or, forbid the sacrilege of even mentioning the holy title, a poet. Merely a backwoods woman, I loved to linger over language and mess around with metaphors. I still do.

With gratitude for everything the people and places of the West have given me, I borrow this line from Wallace Stegner's *The Sound of Mountain Water*: "So if these essays begin in innocence, with a simple-minded love of western landscape and experience, they move toward the attempt . . . to understand what it is one loves, what is special or fragile about it, and how far love alone will take us."

Woman in the Backwoods

December 1974. George Williams College, Downers Grove, Illinois. Standing in front of the student mail slot in the Campus Union building, dressed in an ash-gray wool skirt and blazer, a dove-gray silk blouse, steel-gray high heels, and silver-gray stockings, with a wide-brimmed, slate-gray wool hat that sported a single pheasant feather as decoration, I held a one-page handwritten letter addressed to William F. Atkinson, 59928. That was all the address needed for the note to reach a remote area of northern Montana. Having penned the letter the night before with a nervous hand, I had carried it with me all day. It wasn't long, a few sentences, ending with "I'm coming."

I studied the envelope's eleven-cent postage stamp and the man's name. He and I had exchanged a short, heated barrage of correspondence since fall. I held the message to my heart, said a prayer, and dropped the small white square into the slot. In the split second that it took to let go of a piece of paper, I changed the course of my life.

∾

Just out of my teens, as a third-year student at a private liberal arts college outside Chicago, I had never seen a wild animal except caged in a zoo. I had never camped out or even gone hiking. Every bite of food I had ever eaten had come from a grocery store. Despite being a rank greenhorn, I thought I had the most important ingredient for success—love.

Conceited and selfish as it might seem, I wanted the very best out of my time on earth. I wanted a different lifestyle from the one I had been raised in, one that would nurture me and give me fresh direction and lifelong purpose. As the middle child of an Air Force master sergeant, I had lived in countless places. I had attended fourteen schools in twelve years. I had labored at menial jobs of quiet servitude in places like Denny's Dugout and Yankee Doodle Dandy. Now, in the middle of my junior year of college, having worked in maintenance, the admissions office, and the library, I was restless and discontent. Even the news that I had been accepted as a transfer student into the honors program at the University of Chicago did not quell the panic that surrounded my plan to obtain a master's degree and then a Ph.D. A handsome, charming, and well-educated gentleman had spent the past year squiring me to museums and fine restaurants. When he mentioned marriage, I squirmed away. Desperate for something different, I searched for the crowbar that would pry me out of my ordinary existence and catapult me into something extraordinary.

∾

In *Driftwood Valley*, Theodora Stanwell-Fletcher described her experiences in the backwoods of Canada where she and her biologist-researcher husband spent several years. She wrote, "Credit is given the modern woman who dares the loneliness and hardships of pioneering adventure. But the man who dares to take the woman, be responsible for her well-being and allow his own free movement to be seriously handicapped, deserves as much, if not more, credit than the woman." Theodora knew and I knew that no matter how much I loved the land, yearned for isolation, or longed to become skilled in the outdoors, I needed a man to survive in the wilderness.

More so than a man, a woman lives under the mysterious power of the land. Her life flows in cycles and is guided by seasons. The land and the woman are one, but at age twenty, having been raised on Air Force bases and in suburban settings, I had little understanding of that ancient truth. I had been raised in semi-sterile environments; my hands had never been dirtied by the earth or stained with the blood of a butchered animal. A car transported me along paved streets. Air-conditioning and furnaces protected me from the heat and cold. Insulated windows and doors kept the wind and sun at bay. Through no fault of my own, I was removed from the earth, and after a series of failed love affairs and unfulfilling jobs, my heart demanded that I find a way to go back to the natural cycles now all but forgotten. I longed to live at the most basic level of finding food, shelter, clothing, and companion-ship. I knew of no women strong enough to live a wilderness lifestyle alone, and so I turned toward the idea of finding a man to take me where I needed to go.

~

He called himself Makwi Witco, "Crazy Wolf." After surviving Vietnam, he had sought the peace of inaccessible mountains. I called him Bill. When I first heard about him, he was living far north at the edge of a river flowing from the glacial high country in Canada. Looking for a female companion, he wrote to a new acquaintance back east (meaning the Midwest), "If by chance you should meet a woman who would fit the place in my lodge, by all means say I exist." Bill's friend Steve lived near my college, and his mother worked on campus with me. Knowing my back-to-the-land desire, he brought me the crumpled letter that had been typed on an old manual machine. Steve said, "You better pack your bags."

That night I wrote a short note full of longing and despair to Bill. He replied. So began a fevered three-month correspondence with a stranger thirteen years my senior. Falling in love with men who wrote ardent letters wasn't a novelty for me (I had succumbed to earlier romances when I was seventeen and eighteen), but becoming a mail-ordered companion was, especially when my prospective partner lived twenty-five hundred miles of railroad, small towns, buses, and dreary days away.

∾

Late December 1974. Three A.M. in Fargo, North Dakota. The train had stopped. Snow was piling up outside the foggy windows. People loaded and unloaded luggage, gathered children, and said hellos and good-byes. Next to me, Steve snored lightly. Without his encouragement and guidance, would I ever have had the guts to embark on the journey? A close friend of his was supposed to accompany us west, but she had canceled at the last moment, leaving the pair of us to strike out alone from Chicago's Union Station.

Two youngsters, a brother and a sister, said "So long" to their parents, laughed and giggled, settled into their seats, and sat back happily to begin their trip. They looked far more confident than I felt.

I reread a quote by Erica Jong written in my journal: "Let us not tie ourselves . . . but sail into the unknown of the future, yet not paralyzed into immobility by fear; feeling the fear and yet not letting the fear control us." After twenty-four hours on the train traveling west from Chicago to Montana, I was full of fear and ill at ease. I worried that my decision to try a back-woods lifestyle was idiotic. Had I made a grievous error by quitting college, forsaking my family and friends, and jetti-

soning the plans I had made? What I had left behind was
familiarity; what lay ahead was unknown. I had traded in my
skirts, nylons, and high heels for jeans and flannel shirts. The
heavy pack boots on my feet felt alien. My long hair, pulled
back in braids, felt strange without the usual electric-roller
waves and hairspray. The train moved again, westward into the
black night, across the miles of open country that preceded
the Great Divide.

I envisioned pioneer women in wagons loaded with precious
belongings and children. They too must have felt the uncertainty and fear that comes with change. They followed their
men into a strange new beginning filled with the hope of
something better, willed by the joy that comes when the future
looms with promise instead of despair. Kindred spirit, I had
left behind the city's desperation, and I hoped I was going to
the promise of a simpler life. Somewhere to the west, perhaps
sitting on his horse atop a snow-covered bluff looking east, Bill
waited for me. I stared out at the darkness, pressing my flushed
face to the cool window.

∽

Leaving the Chicago suburbs and two decades of city-girl
thinking was no easy matter. I began by disposing of all
unnecessary possessions. I left my favorite books, childhood
mementos, and fine clothing in the care of my older sister. I
stopped wearing makeup and curling my hair. I quit shaving
my legs and showering twice a day. Giving up candy, soft
drinks, alcohol, and prepackaged items, I tried to approximate
my diet to the meat, vegetables, and bread I thought I would
have in the backwoods. I tried to imagine the kind of place I
would live in and thought Bill's cabin might look like the big
ranch house called the Ponderosa on the TV show *Bonanza*.
With no domestic skills, I felt apprehensive about the things
I did not know how to do. And if I lacked housekeeping knowl-

edge, my outdoor skills were nonexistent. The idea of handling an ax or a gun was as foreign to me as the idea of trekking across the craters of the moon.

I had little in hand: my flagging confidence and a stuffed backpack. Clothing and a few sundries were crammed in with a ream of paper and twenty-five dollars in cash left over after I bought my train ticket. It was not much with which to begin a new life. The train, squeaking and grinding on worn rails, pushed on into the next day.

∾

Whitefish, Montana, was a fairyland cloaked in snow that glistened with lights reflecting each tiny perfect crystal falling in slow motion in the late evening air. Thirty-six hours on the train had dampened my enthusiasm for adventure. All I wanted was a place to sleep. Steve helped me shoulder my heavy pack, and we stumbled through the roadside drifts. Vehicles churned along the icy streets, the ching-chinging of tire chains a new song to my ears. The water in the motel room ran cold, but the bed was warm and I slept well, dreaming of being on the train with the countryside rolling by forever.

A small van that carried the mail took us on as passengers. In Kalispell, Dave, a friend of Bill's, met us at the bus station. He and his wife, Robin, provided Steve and me with a place to sleep and meals for several days until Dave could find time from his busy schedule as a nurseryman to transport us eighty-six miles north to the cabin on the river.

I was nervous and exhausted. The only thing I remembered about those days of waiting was Robin talking about Robinson Jeffers and that I threw up repeatedly in the back yard. My only desire was to get to my destination and stop worrying about meeting Bill.

Val Halla

When the day came to head upcountry, Steve, Dave, and
I crowded into the cab of Dave's four-wheel-drive truck. I
watched the winter roads slip by until we left the towns of
Kalispell and Columbia Falls behind. The freshly plowed highway turned into snow-packed secondary roads. Houses and
buildings disappeared, then fences, then telephone and electric
poles. Soon there were no other roads, no other vehicles. We
traveled on a one-lane trace sided by ten-foot-high snow
berms. A thick lodgepole forest loomed on both sides. A narrow scrap of dingy sky stretched above. At noon we passed Polebridge, Bill's mailing address, which was nothing more than a
store with a post office and a solitary gas pump. Bucking snow
for twenty-six more miles, we reached the end of the semi-
open road at the Canadian border.

Dave commented that we were lucky the road had been
plowed the week before and fresh snow had not blocked our
passage. From the widened spot where we parked, a dim trail
led downriver. We followed it, lengthening our steps in thigh-

deep snow to match the stride of the horses that had traveled the path before us. Extreme fatigue had made my legs shaky by the time a barn came into view, and we had traveled only a quarter of a mile. Visible through the pines, smoke drifted from the cabin stovepipe. Bill was either home or close by.

Surprised by unexpected guests, the horses snorted and raced away, throwing clouds of snow into the air. Curious, the goats came to the barn door, peered out, and then pranced around to make our acquaintance. Terrified, I gamely tried to make friends with the largest, whose name I knew from Bill's letters: Kimikoi. A giant LaMancha doe, she reared on her hind legs and charged several times, a sure sign that she usually got the attention she demanded. We trooped up the narrow trail with the menagerie of goats and horses following. At the sound of our approach, a handful of cats crawled out of the woodpile to mew and rub against our snow-covered legs. Dave pounded on the split-plank portal and bellowed out "Hello the camp."

The door flew open, and Bill's buckskin-clad figure filled the frame. "Well, I'll be goddamned. I've been expecting you half-whites. Who's this?" he asked, gesturing to me. Certain that Bill did not know me, I hid like a child behind Steve's back. Then Bill laughed, punched me on the arm, and crushed me in a giant bear hug.

The cabin smelled of wood smoke. Above each window and door, huge elk racks held rifles. Hides and furs covered the walls. Hunting and trapping paraphernalia lay on tables. An old upright piano stood in the corner by a window. Across from it, an ancient typewriter on a small table marked the place where Bill had spent evenings typing letters to me. A large wood heat stove dominated the living area, while a white-enameled wood range heated the kitchen. Two propane lights hung from the ceiling, one at each end of the long room. Kerosene lamps stood on counters and cupboards.

A pot of black-eyed peas was boiling on the stovetop. A large pitcher of fresh goat's milk and a loaf of homemade bread rested on the table. My stomach churned. I fought down the feeling that I would never be able to eat without throwing up. Bill dished up our lunch, and I sat with the others and nibbled to be polite. A big white cat leapt to my lap and curled up to purr. "Kriega," Bill said. "He likes you. That's a good sign." A thin stream of the tom's contented drool dampened my thigh.

Bill talked with great enthusiasm and in a booming voice. Dave roared back at him. Their exuberant laughter made the windows shake. Quiet, Steve sat and grinned. I perched on the edge of the straight-backed chair and listened, saying nothing. In a foreign realm, my first challenge was to learn the language and customs. My second would be to not make a fool of myself too soon.

~

Built about 1919, Bill's cabin was called a homesteader story-and-a-half. It was constructed of huge tamarack (larch) logs, some of which were more than two feet in diameter. The lower floor combined the kitchen and living area. The upper floor was reserved for sleeping and storage. Long and narrow, the four windows filtered in enough winter light to make the dim atmosphere vaguely gray. No visible plumbing meant no indoor facilities. Embarrassed, but in pain from clenching my thighs together, I finally asked about a bathroom. Bill led me to a window and pointed to an outhouse around the back. I ventured outside, my tentative steps crunching on the packed snow trail. I paused to listen to a silence broken only by the song of the river that flowed between icy banks fifty feet away.

A two-holer, the outhouse had bare board walls and a bench with oval cutouts plus the luxury of store-bought toilet seats. On a nail hung a circle of carpet that matched the size of the seats—a device, I later learned, to keep butt flesh from freezing to the hard plastic on below-zero days. I slipped inside and closed the door. There was no light and no way to lock the door with the latch on the outside. I had no choice but to allow it to swing open on large hinges to reveal an astounding view of the high peaks of Glacier National Park. A coffee can with a plastic lid housed a half-used roll of toilet paper that had earlier been given a lacy edge by gnawing mice.

When I returned to the cabin, Bill said, "Three squares a day. Not meals—toilet paper. You have to learn how to conserve, because once the road snows shut, there is no way out. Not for supplies. Not for anything."

༄

Late that afternoon, Dave waved good-bye and hiked back out to his rig, leaving Bill, Steve, and me alone with the goats, cats, and horses in the quiet silver glow of dusk. We stayed up late as the fire burned low, with Bill and Steve arguing philosophical differences along with which rifle caliber was best suited for what kind of game. When Bill suggested that it was time to turn in, he told Steve to take the spare room and tossed him a black bear robe to ward off the night chill.

Alone with me in front of a long slab table laden with skulls, skins, knives, and intricate antler engravings, Bill lit a candle. He said, "I don't want a fishwife or a scullery maid. I don't need a bunch of hyped-up vows or the entanglement of chains. I want a woman who will complement me and honor the lifestyle I've carved out here."

Mute, I nodded my head.

"Did you bring the medicine bag I sent you?" he asked. I pulled the small white leather pouch hanging from a buckskin thong from the inside of my shirt.

"Did you open it?" he asked.

"No," I said, studying the intricate knot that sealed the opening shut. "Was I supposed to?"

He laughed low and warm. "No, Little Fawn. How could you have known the power of what I tucked inside? You have passed the first of many tests."

Bill took the medicine bag from around my neck, deftly untied the knot, and extracted a tiny hand-carved ivory thunderbird with a drilled hole for an eye. He wore one just like it around his neck. With a magician's sleight of hand, he produced another buckskin thong, threaded the thunderbird, and tied it around my neck. "Be certain you honor the man who took the time to make this for you."

He led me up the stairs in the dark. The window over the bed was open, and a skift of snow had drifted on top of the elk robe covering. Outside, the river's muffled roar sounded under the ice. A coyote called. Then another. Then a full chorus. "They've come to welcome you," Bill said, stripping down. "I can tell you are afraid, and that fear will eat you alive. Come to bed."

Shivering, I undressed and slid under the elk robe onto the soft fur of beaver pelts. I did not wish to have sex, but I wanted to make love. How could I make that clear? Everything inside me burned to know the strange beast of a man who lay beside me, his long hair and beard indecipherable from the texture of the animal's skins. How could I let Bill know how fragile I was, that I needed him to be tender? He turned on his side to look at me. With a perfect tenor voice he began to sing, "Oh my love, my darling, I've hungered for your touch, a long lonely time."

∾

Within a couple of weeks, the men fell into a violent argument after Steve ate one of Bill's carefully saved oranges. Steve took me aside and pleaded with me to leave with him. He didn't think it would be wise or safe for me to stay with Bill. He explained that Bill's outburst was a sign of abnormal behavior.

Though upset, I noticed nothing unusual in Bill's tantrum. I had been raised by a demanding military-minded father with a terrible temper. Still, I wondered whether Bill had orchestrated the drama to get Steve to leave. It was clear that Steve harbored special feelings for me. Perhaps Bill did not want any competition for my heart. Hurt and angry, Steve snowshoed out to hitch a ride back to town with the mailman. I saw no one except Bill until spring.

A Man Alone

In one of the letters Bill had written to me, he said, "The setting sun was gone, but blood red shone on the snowy peaks across the frozen meadow as I stopped to watch. With a full mountain lion for a cape and the heat of the horse beneath me, I sat warm and silent. The north wind keened a lonesome sound and set the eagle feather in my mink hat to whirring. Gone was all else in the world except the red sky slowly turning to lavender, mauve, and then pink. To the north and west—mountains. To the south and east—mountain peaks. Mine! A world of isolation, stillness, and beauty beyond my wildest dreams."

No wonder I fell in love with him and the landscape he called home before I ever even met him. That world where sunsets colored the peaks west of the Great Divide remained much as it had been a hundred years earlier—a wilderness stronghold with miles of timbered mountainsides and open meadows, a place of supreme, pristine beauty where a glacial river tumbled out of the Northern Rockies. Through that country Bill rode, the tracks of his spotted stallion crisscrossing those of elk and moose. He considered himself to be a lone man, one who had chosen long ago to be independent and free.

When I met Bill, he had already seen ten winters come and go along the old Kootenai Indian trail adjacent to present-day Glacier National Park. At fourteen, he had dreamed of hunting camps and distant places. At eighteen, the day after his high school graduation, he left his Florida home and headed north to what he and Thomas Jefferson called the "shining mountains" of Montana. He spent his first winter alone in a solitary cabin beneath the shadow of a snow-capped peak. Several years later, his dream of a life on the land still strong, he worked as the roving guard of the Bob Marshall Wilderness. With a saddle horse and a pack mule, he rode the high trails, hearing the wind's song in the pines and smelling the cleanness of mountain mornings. His dreams were interrupted, however, when he joined the Navy to avoid being drafted. Fifteen months of service in Vietnam convinced Bill that man's inhumanity to man was a stark, hellish reality. He swore never to be involved in such senselessness again.

In 1968 he returned to the mountains of Montana. He wandered the Devil's Kitchen country off the Missouri River Canyon and later traveled north. As autumn faded into the first snows of winter, Bill arranged with a landowner to live in an abandoned homesteader cabin on the bank of the Northfork of the Flathead. The locals called the place Moose City. Bill called it Val Halla: home of returning warriors. With a rifle, an ax, and a crosscut saw, he began to carve out an existence. When that winter melted into spring, Bill became fully aware of the incomparable value of the domain he had found. Miles of unbroken and unfenced land stretched from the cabin in every direction. The wild ones, although not as abundant as in earlier times, remained. Every major predator and prey species was represented, from the hulking grizzly to the lowliest snowshoe hare. His hunting and trapping boyhood in Florida served him well, and he had no trouble mastering his homemade knives

and tomahawks. On snowshoes he followed the game trails
and learned the patterned routines of the animals. In the late
spring, when the ruffed grouse drummed for mates, he hand-
dug a garden and planted a variety of root crops and herbs.
As the days lengthened and the deer returned to the lower
meadows, he found time to ride or run the river rapids in his
canoe. When the smell of the drying leaves and curing grass
signaled the end of summer, he cut down fire-charred tamarack snags for wood. He trekked up nearby creek drainages to
search for huckleberries, strawberries, and wild mint. While
the neighboring beaver gathered willows for winter feed, Bill
harvested his garden. He home-canned or dried the produce
and stored it in the root cellar he had dug. Before the north
wind stole the golden leaves from the cottonwood trees and the
snows came again, he traveled into town to trade engravings he
had carved on elk ivory for staple foods like wheat, honey, salt,
beans, potatoes, and fruit. After snowfall, when the road closed
and summer folk left the lower valley, he killed an elk and a
bear to provide enough meat for an entire year. He canned the
forequarters of the elk and hung the hindquarters in an old ice-
house to freeze solid during the cold nights. Every evening he
sawed off a thick steak with a bow saw and grilled it over the
open eye of flame on his wood cook stove. The bear's meat was
cured and smoked, and its fat rendered for cooking grease and
making soap. The hides of both animals were fleshed, stretched
over wood frames, and tanned into robes for sleeping.

Although Bill had experimented with different methods of
tanning with chemicals, he had long sought to produce buckskin that would be durable but soft. Through a chance acquaintance, he heard about the lost American Indian art of tanning a
hide by softening it with the animal's own brains. He spent an
entire winter working with the braintanning process until he
succeeded. He taught himself how to cut and stitch skins and
pelts into utilitarian garments. Then he taught himself how to
decorate his shirts and moccasins with quills and beads.

In 1970, determined to learn the secrets of hand forging, Bill
traveled to the River of No Return in the Salmon Wilderness
to seek the advice of the old mountain man Sylvan Hart. Hart
shared several techniques with him, and Bill returned home to
discover the enchantment of sparks flying from a blacksmith's
forge. He made knives out of high-quality quarter-inch tool
steel blanks for his own use, for gutting, skinning, and butchering big game animals. Each blade was finished with an antler
handle complete with finger grips and a specially engraved
antler sheath. Using tools he designed himself, Bill also taught
himself to polish, carve, and engrave the rosette bases of deer,
elk, and moose antlers.

For five years, the pattern of Bill's life changed little. He
walked and snowshoed, lived and learned. In the summer of
1973, he traded a bobcat engraving and $150 he had saved for a
sorrel mare and her bay colt. He left his northern mountains
and rode south, headed for the Yellowstone. At Cherry Creek,
he lost the packhorse he had borrowed to poisoned grain. To
go on, he accepted the loan of an unbroke molly mule that had
him picking up scattered gear for a couple of days. When she
tumbled off a cliff in the Spanish Peaks, Bill scrambled down to
rescue her, and she knew she had a friend. With her gashed legs
washed and treated, she meekly walked the remaining forty
miles to their destination.

When I arrived on Bill's doorstep in January 1975, he had
been alone for a long time, except for the company of his goats,
a flock of chickens, the green-broke bay colt, Ahkee (named
for the piercing scream of the sparrow hawk), the sorrel mare,
Jubilee, heavy with another foal, a glass-eyed paint gelding
named Jeremiah, and the coyotes who howled a nightly chorus
outside his loft bedroom window.

I did not know then the difference between aloneness and
loneliness. Nor did I understand how those states of being both
save and scar a man forever.

There Were No Women

While I sat huddled on the train en route from Chicago to
Montana that early-winter morning, many thoughts and worries had scurried through my mind: Would the man I loved,
but knew only through his ardent letters, like me? Would Bill
think I was pretty? Would I be tough enough to live in his wilderness world? Would I need money, and if I did, how would
I earn any cash living eighty-some miles from town? Could I
learn to cook, sew, split wood, hunt, and butcher? What would
I do about tampons and birth control? Could I live without a
telephone or plumbing? How would I find books to read? Yet
the one thing that never crossed my mind was whether there
would be other women in my life.

The first few silent months I lived on the Northfork, I never
saw or spoke to another woman. My mother and sisters wrote
to me. My friend Guynn, a wild-running artist-actress whose
unconventional ways had instilled in me the personal courage
to quit school, wrote and sent me four hand-painted soup
mugs and two packets of sweet-smelling bath salts. I tucked

them away in my underwear drawer because there was no
bathtub and no way to take a bath. I wrote to the woman who
ran the post office–grocery store at Polebridge and slipped my
last ten-dollar bill in the envelope. She sent me two boxes of
tampons wrapped in brown paper via the mail. When the tampons ran out, I folded washrags and pinned them into my panties. When they soiled, I rinsed them in the icy river, scalded
them with boiling water from the teakettle, and hung them
over the wood stove to dry.

I counted the days on the calendar carefully, and those times
when my period came late, I lived in mortal fear of being preg-
nant, terrified that Bill, who was extremely stern in his demand
that he wanted no children, would cast me aside. When the
first spots of blood finally appeared, weeks late, I was so relieved that I bore the accompanying pain without complaint.
It would be twenty years before I learned from the surgeon
who performed my hysterectomy that I had suffered through
several early-onset miscarriages.

When folks snowmachined to our door to visit late that first
spring, I had turned so painfully shy that I scurried upstairs
and hid until they left. When the snow melted and the road
dried out, we made our first trip to town in an old pickup, but
I felt clumsy and unable to speak to anyone.

The waitress at the diner said hello and smiled at me, but
I ducked my head, ashamed of my simple braids, my faded
jeans, and my chore coat that smelled like goats and manure. I
often thought of Madge, the woman who had lived in the log
cabin on the river years before. Bill had told me that she cut off
her hair, jammed on a hat, and dressed like a man. She cussed
and chewed tobacco, and she had a habit of marrying her hired
hands so she wouldn't have to pay them wages. When they got
disgusted with her and left, she just married another. She outlived all of them until she dropped dead of a heart attack in
front of the old wood range in the kitchen. I would stand in the
spot where Madge died and gain an uncanny sense of strength

from knowing that not only had she survived the isolation, she had thrived. Plus, she had apparently figured out how to handle men, a skill that I suspected would never be mine.

In bits and pieces, through scattered tatters of gossip, I heard the grisly story floating around the valley about the girl Bill had had when he was sent to Vietnam. He had written to her the whole time he was there. Their letters were saved in a locked steel box by the bed. Her clothing still rested in the dresser drawers, and her rings still lay in a small dish by the washbasin. Rumor had it that after a few years together after his return from 'Nam, she simply disappeared. The strong, unveiled hint was that Bill had killed her and buried the body in a crevasse high in the mountains.

And then there was the oblong wooden box under the bed in the room where I slept by myself. I seldom slept with Bill; he wouldn't allow me to. An uneasy sleeper, he retained a warrior's hypervigilance. Plus, the night burdened him with troubled dreams and a restless mind. He preferred to sleep alone under a pile of wool blankets and a bear robe. He liked to open the window above him so that the frigid air and snow drifted in over his head. His room stayed too cold for me. Even after lovemaking, when I longed for snuggles and cuddles, the warmth of connection, he sent me away to the room where the box waited in the dark.

Early on, Bill had forbidden me to open that box. He had given me orders that I was never to touch it. The rumor haunted me. I imagined the girl who came before me cold and rigid in that damn makeshift coffin. Finally, unable to stand not knowing, but terrified to investigate for myself, I insisted that Bill open it for me. He had a sadistic gleam in his eyes when he complied with my request to pull the box from under the bed. He pried off the lid to reveal case-skinned, perfectly hand-tanned hides of otter, ermine, fox, mink, marten, wolverine, lynx, lion, and coyote. "What did you think was in here?" he asked. When I told him, he laughed, thoroughly

enjoying the joke, savoring the notion that the valley folk had
pegged him as being crazier than even he admitted to being.

Sex and love remained an insane conundrum for me. If I had
had a close woman friend to talk with, perhaps I would not
have been so mixed up about what constituted a healthy relationship. I thought I wanted to be married and have a family. I
wrote my first name and Bill's last name together over and over
again on pieces of brown-bag paper. I loved playing with the
idea of Ms. and Mrs., but if Bill walked into the room, I
crumpled the dreams in a hurry and burned them in the stove.
Marriage was a subject he would not discuss except to say that
wives had ruined every man he had ever met, including his
father.

Brief visits and occasional meetings with other females
helped me keep my sanity. Pixie-like Annie Chappell, who had
spent a few months with Bill the previous summer, came in
April of the first year and stayed a week. An artist named
Jammy lived eight miles away on Trail Creek with her boy-
friend, Mark. She signed her paintings with a double bleeding
heart, and she birthed her first child one winter night in her
remote cabin. A young Mormon housewife, Marlene, who
always seemed to be nursing a new baby, lived twelve miles
downriver. The American border guard's wife, Irene, stayed
summers in the crossing station. She once fixed butter beans
and ham and cornbread with maple syrup and invited me to
come for supper when Bill left me alone. There were women
in town that I came to know, like Flo, Liz, Valerie, Noelle,
Nancy, and Jean, but I never overcame my shyness enough to
ask them anything about late periods, horrible cramps, or the
long weeks of weakness and fatigue that followed. We talked
about men, but mostly in the context of why they were so difficult to understand and impossible to love. Even in the 1970s,
the subject of sex, not to mention the ever-elusive orgasm,
wasn't broached.

The Northfork was a man's world, Bill's world. There was no room for girlish sentiment or feminine sympathy. One morning I spilled the milk. The colt kicked me. Bill yelled at me after I burned yet another batch of biscuits. Then Ahkee dumped me and stepped on my ankle as we floundered in the deep drift that hid the mailbox. My fierce resolve melted into a trickle of painful tears that froze on my cheeks. Returning to the cabin, I tossed the mail on the table with an angry, dismissive gesture that I hoped said "I'm leaving." Bill never looked up from his work at a desk by the window.

Re-zipping my coat, I hiked out to the buried road. Better said, I shoved and plowed and fell and sobbed until I shook with exhaustion. My ankle throbbed and shot red-hot needles up my leg. I looked up to see that I had made it only a half-mile past the mailbox. More than twenty-five miles of stumbling ahead remained. Two choices stared me down: I could keep going, with no hope of ever getting to Polebridge, or I could fight my way back to the cabin. Furious at my own fear of pain or possible death, I turned for the only place I knew to call home.

Hearing me wailing upstairs, Bill found me huddled in a corner under the window. He stood there polishing a piece of antler and stared at me. He said, "If you're going to cry, you might as well go home to your mother." Then he walked out. He didn't hear me mumble under my breath, "You son of a bitch, if I could get out of this goddamned place, that's right where I'd go." He had slapped me once for talking back to him, and I was not stupid enough to risk his hair-trigger temper again. Too ignorant, young, and afraid to know that love didn't mean I had to keep trying to find a way to stay, I stopped crying. I blew my nose and stomped downstairs to fix supper.

Why did I choose to stay in such circumstances? Pride. Stubbornness. An attempt to show that I was tough enough to make it in a man's world? What was I trying to prove? And to whom? What did I hope to gain? If I stuck it out, did I believe that Bill would come to love me as I loved him? If I had had some older woman to confide in, could she have convinced me to give up my ridiculous quest? Years later, trying to explain my experience to my own heart, I wrote: "Mail came up but twice a week when the dirt road could stay open. No telephone to salve the stretch of endless days with a silent man, the nearest neighbor miles away, and there just were no women. Morning and evening chores to do, planting and gardening in the spring, harvest and canning in the fall, no helping hands to ease the load, no laughing smiles or teasing fights because there were no women. In memory my mother's face, or those of sisters, aunts, and friends, in magazines those feminine dreams of playing house and beauty shop turned so lost and left behind because there were no women. So I sang to goats, hugged the cats, conversed with the sad-eyed dog, whispered words to shaggy horses, held close a pine tree's roughened bark, wept silly tears, hurt and harsh, because there were no women. Children came, barely conceived, and cursed before believed in, dark red rushes slipping away in wadded sheets and bloodied fear left me shivering to wash alone because there were no women. I was more tired than lonely, more lonely than afraid, my heart turned hard, my hands grew raw, my soul dried and shriveled—near to dying, way past crying because in all those long gone years there just never were any women."

Why hadn't I confided my problems to my mother or my sisters? Why did I keep my struggles inside? Why did I hide my pain? Was I afraid that someone would try to talk me out of my self-imposed imprisonment? What did I hope to gain by enduring everything alone? I would be halfway through the average female life span before I had the opportunity to truly know the value of another woman's comforting hand and listening ear.

Knot Tying

I was never much good at knots, except, of course, shoelaces, which I learned to tie in kindergarten with quiet expertise. I guess I felt that tying my shoes was knowledge enough. Besides, I spent my youth in places like the Philippines, Texas, and Hawaii, where I went barefoot or wore flip-flops; so knot-tying, on shoelaces or otherwise, did not concern me until I came west.

On Bill's homestead, I soon found out that knots were needed for everything: tying up goats for milking, securing a rabbit cage door, retying the twine on a bale of hay, knotting a thread for sewing on a button. In my placid ignorance, I figured a knot was a knot. I could do laces. I mastered my pack boots. Who cared if my final product was a square or a granny?

Bill tried with endless patience to explain a square knot to me: right over left, left over right. A very successful, stout, and easy-to-untie knot. Only an idiot tied a granny that could tighten up into an unsightly mess that could not be untied. Bill was a knot expert: bowline, Turk's head, slipknot, half hitch, clove hitch, overhand, sheepshank, surgeon's knot, clinch knot, double bowknot. He knew knots for tying boats, tying horses, securing packs on a saddle, and fastening down tarps. He knew knots for hoisting up carcasses, and for putting tiny stitches in wounded flesh. I tested his tolerance with my ignorance and inability to learn. Everything I attempted to tie either came untied within minutes or seized into a welter that refused to be untied. Bill's lesson on tying a horse so the rope would not tighten up if the horse reared back against the halter went like this: "Make a loop. That's the rabbit hole. The end of the rope is the rabbit. The rabbit comes out of his hole, gets scared, and runs around and dives back into his hole. Got it?" he asked. "Uh, sure, I guess," I replied.

But I didn't get it. Foolishly, I didn't care. I never had to tie up a horse anyway. I rode where I needed to go, turned around, and came back home, so it was no problem.

Then came the day in late fall of my first year on the river when a young man named Tom hiked into our place. He was wintering downstream about eight miles at the Homeplace Ranch, and he had heard that Bill was a master at tanning hides. Tom wanted to learn how to make buckskin. Bill's satisfied grin said, "Ah! An apprentice to help with the grunt work." Tom stayed and visited with us all afternoon. Bill concluded that the greenhorn had guts and invited him to stay for a couple of weeks. In exchange for helping flesh and grain deer hides, Bill would teach Tom the fine art of braintanning buckskin the old Indian way.

As we ate supper, Tom said he should be getting home. He would pick up some gear and come back in a day or two. "Why don't you take a horse of mine, and you can be there and back again in no time?" Bill offered.

Tom hesitated. He had already hiked nine miles upcountry that morning by following the road that had recently been

plowed by a logging crew to the border. I wondered if he had
had much experience with horses.

"Take Laurie with you," Bill said. "She loves a chance to ride,
and the horses know her." I could imagine Tom thinking about
how much more gear he could pack on a horse than he could
carry on his back. He rose to the unspoken challenge. We all
knew that Bill was testing his mettle, to see just how far he
would reach for the chance to learn an important backwoods
skill.

"Well, sure," Tom answered politely. "Okay, we'll do that,
and thanks."

Bill and Tom continued visiting while I hurried through
dishes and chores and dressed warmly. With the sun setting, the
night air promised to be cold. We had about two feet of snow
on the ground, but once we reached the plowed road, the horses
would be able to move at a long trot and cover the miles.

Out at the barn, we saddled up the old paint, Jeremiah, for
Tom, and I put my small saddle on Ahkee, the three-year-old
just-broke colt. We left Jubilee in the barn so she would not
follow. As the horses picked their way across the packed trail
over the meadow, the last sunlight faded from view. We walked
through a dark fringe of lodgepole timber, up a steep bank and
over the berm, then onto the snow-packed road. Tom did not
seem particularly comfortable on Jere. He sat tense and alert,
but I could tell he had ridden before by the way he kept his
weight even in the stirrups and neck-reined with care.

To make time, we alternately trotted the horses, then slowed
to a walk so they could blow and we could talk. A nearly full
moon appeared, and our trail was marked by bright splashes
of silvery light and the shadows of the pines. In the soft breeze
that came out of the east, we heard an occasional tree squeak.
I told Tom the story about my first week with Bill, when I had
tried very hard to figure out which animal or bird made that
elusive sound. To my embarrassment and to Bill's barely

restrained delight, he finally told me that the noise was only tree branches touching in the wind. Except for the crunch of horse hooves on snow, the creak of saddle leather, and our half-whispered voices, tree squeaks were the only sound.

Two hours passed, and we were both stiff with cold despite the exercise needed to stay in the saddle. If I had been alone, I would have gotten off and walked to increase my dwindling circulation, but with Tom along I was too proud to dismount. I wanted to prove that I was tough enough to stay in the saddle. Once past Trail Creek, Tom began to study the left-hand side of the road, looking for the mailbox that would mark the trail through the timber to the ranch he was caretaking. The moon danced between huge clouds. One moment, vibrant light drenched us; the next, darkness swamped us.

Spotting the mailbox, we climbed down and led the horses off the road into the timber to tie them safely away from any unlikely but happenstance traffic. The idea of a snowmachine or a truck coming by seemed ridiculous, yet we wanted to take no chances on losing our mounts.

Because the snow lay belly deep in the timber, the horses would have to stay there. Traveling for Tom and me would be much easier on foot in the dark on the packed snowshoe trail, which would hold our weight. I picked out a tall, straight six-inch tree that sported a handy stub of a branch at about eye level so the halter rope would not slide down the trunk and allow the colt to get tangled. I tied my knot. Not right. I tried again. Still wrong. In the semidarkness, doing things by feel, I tried again. With Jere tied, Tom waited. I threw some loops, snugged it up, and said a prayer. I loosened my cinch a couple of notches and joined Tom. He had taken his snowshoes off from behind the saddle and held them in one hand. There was no need for them on a trail that had softened in the afternoon sun and then iced tight in the frigid air. He hid them out of sight behind some dog-hair jack pine.

My limbs were stiff. My mouth barely opened when I tried to speak. I had long since lost feeling in my feet, and the sharp tingles of returning circulation ached as we hiked slow and silent through the dense trees. Tom led the way, stopping only when the moon slid behind a cloud and he could not see his way ahead. Two great horned owls, alerted to our uncommon presence, began to who-who to each other as they drifted from treetop to treetop and marked our passage. Shivers itched up my spine from the eerie calls.

It was a winding downhill mile to the river flat; then the timber thinned, allowing moonlight to pour over us unobstructed. Weathered homestead buildings stretched out like sleeping seniors. Tom led me past several large structures and onto the porch of a little cabin. He told me that he had picked the smallest place so it would be easy for him to heat with the wood he had hand-sawn in the summer months. We stumbled inside to pure blackness. Tom felt around for the box of matches on the counter. He struck one on the cast-iron top of the wood cook stove and reached for a Coleman lamp. The tiny kitchen glowed in golden light. Tom crumpled newspaper and stacked kindling to get a fire going, then put on a kettle of water to make hot drinks. While he fished around in drawers and cupboards for clothing, a sleeping bag, books, and other necessities, I took off my pack boots, put the felt liners and my socks in the warming oven, and set my frozen feet on the stove box to soak up the heat.

By the time Tom finished packing, we had swilled down a cup of cocoa and munched a handful of graham crackers. In a half-hour's time we were back on the trail leading up to the road where we had left the horses. Tom had a small backpack and his guitar case in hand, and I carried his down sleeping bag. The wind had risen. Although the air current had warmed the temperature, it retained a sharp glacial bite. I was glad that it buffeted our backs and did not hit us head on. The tall pines swayed and moaned; tree squeaks cried from far and near. The owls were gone, and I wondered where they had flown to hunt their night mice.

I sighed with relief when Jere's paint hide gleamed white through the dark timber. He nickered and pawed the tramped snow at the base of the tree where he stood tied.

"Hi, old son," I murmured. "Yes, we're going home now."

"Hey, Ahkee," I said, sliding around Jere—only to find nothing there.

"Shit," I said.

"What?" asked Tom.

"Ahkee's gone."

Crazy questions swirled: Would he go back the right way and head for home and not downcountry? Would the loosened saddle slip under his belly? Would the dragging lead rope catch on something? Would he try to drop and roll with the saddle on his back?

"Bill is going to kill me," I said.

Tom said nothing.

I took a deep breath and said, "Just stay here a minute."

I waited until the moon peeked through the clouds, then I scanned the stomped ground for Ahkee's exit tracks. I followed them out to the road and scouted to make sure no horse tracks turned downcountry. When I was positive he had gone north, headed home to his ma, I returned and told Tom to strap on his gear and mount up. "I'll walk," I said.

"No," he insisted. "You are the lady. You should ride and I should walk."

"No," I persisted. "You've already walked nine miles and ridden nine and walked two more. You're a damn sight more tired than I am."

"Maybe," he said, "but my butt's rubbed raw. I'd much rather walk than ride."

We compromised by tying all his gear on Jere and headed up the road walking, with Tom leading the paint.

The wind alternately cried, then died. The setting moon
gave up its hide-and-seek game with the clouds. We were left
with dim starlight and the fairly smooth track beneath our
feet. Cold and tired, neither of us spoke except to mumble,
"You okay?"

Jere plodded behind, his head low. I listened for Ahkee and
squinted into the dark, hoping I would not miss some glimpse
of him tangled in the brush. The miles crawled past in a grad-
ual, slow uphill climb toward home.

From far across the meadow, I strained to see the barn. I
longed to whistle for Ahkee and hear a whinny in return, but
I feared waking Bill and revealing the dark secret of my blun-
der. The shape of the log barn grew out of the night. The mare
heard us coming and nickered from inside. The faint sound
of the goats' bells rang as they rose from their beds. Ahkee
appeared from around the corner of the corral, his muffled
huh-huh sounding around the mouthful of grass hay he had
filched from the goats' manger. I eased up, talking softly, until
I got hold of his lead rope. I cussed him out in a whisper for
being a no-good stupid greenhorn colt that didn't know
enough to stay where he was tied. Making certain that his saddle was in place and his hackamore still looped and tied on the
horn, I led him in a circle to make sure he was not lame. Then
I said a silent prayer—not only for the colt's well-being, but for
the fact that I would not have to face Bill with the news that
I had lost or injured his prize possession.

Tom and I unsaddled the horses and turned all three of them
out. We stayed long enough to watch Jere and Ahkee roll in the
snow, then we hiked up the long path to the cabin. The river
roared below the ice-edged banks. Cottonwood branches
clicked in the wind.

"Stay here," I told Tom in the woodshed. "Let me get a lamp
lit."

When the wick flared to life, I reopened the door for Tom.
He tossed his gear in a corner. "Go ahead and unroll your bed

on the couch," I said as I checked the fire and added another large split of buckskin tamarack to the dying coals.

"Goodnight, Tom," I said. He reached out and touched my arm. "Don't worry," he said. "I won't tell Bill." I kissed him on the cheek and headed upstairs.

Bill heard me and rolled over in bed. "Everything all right?" he asked.

"Yes," I said. "Just cold and tired. We heard horned owls."

"Hmmmm," he complained as I crawled under the blankets. "I'll just stay a little while," I said. I settled against his warmth, relieved that I did not have to tell him about the long walk home.

I closed my eyes: the rabbit came out of her hole, got scared, ran around, and dived back into her hole again—but which way did she run? Did she come out of the hole first? Or dive back into the hole? Did she go left or right? How did the rabbit know which way was correct? Why didn't she run away? Why did she keep going back down into the black hole?

Hanging in Balance

Because I was not born to the land, I came with the idea that I would stay one winter season. I ended up staying for life. From the outset, for me, it was never easy. I had nothing to lose, but I also had everything to learn. I had to start over, begin again. Every lesson I learned, from splitting wood and carrying water to birthing and butchering, came hard for me, and the hardest lesson of all was death.

The eye of the hen was dark, unblinking, and ringed with gold. Every tiny burnt-red feather on her head perfectly sculpted, she was stretched out on the wood block. The concentric age rings in the old and weathered wood wove circles around and around her head like a haloed aura of light. Gripping her stiff legs, my left hand was festooned with homemade bandages, badges of honor earned while learning to split kindling. My right hand held the big double-bitted ax aloft and trembling. The hen had shared my attic room for several weeks, penned up with food and water and warmth to help her heal from the brutal pecking she had received while cooped in with the flock. Now, fat and well, she was destined for the dinner table. For over a month we had been eating smoked bear ham and elk steaks sawn whole from a frozen haunch. Chicken would be a welcome change. "Don't swing too hard. The weight of the ax will chop through her neck," Bill coached. I hesitated. "Just toss her into the snow." I let the ax fall. I felt weak and sick but remembered thinking later that the plucking and gutting was far tougher work than the killing.

Snowed in, my first months on the land were often desolate and lonely. My only contact with the outside world came with the mail when the four-wheel-drive postman's rig could make it as far as the border. Pride helped me stay. I learned to cook on the wood stove. I split wood and carried water. I washed clothes by hand, rinsed them in the ice-bound river, and hung them to freeze in the bitter night air. All dank air and darkness, its timbered roof covered with thousands of hibernating daddy longlegs, the root cellar impressed me. The root crops stored in bins of sand and the hundreds of jars of fruit, vegetables, and jam reassured me that we would not go hungry. Once I learned how to milk the goats and fork out hay for the horses, I enjoyed the early morning and late evening routine of chores. Always tired, always sore, I often faltered, but the silence and the soothing sound of the river sustained me.

By spring, now a hand of sorts, I continually busied myself with chores or cooking and cleaning. When I had time, I learned to bead, and I read or wrote letters to family and friends. The air was pungent with manure and earth smells when the snow left. The river ran high, mud-rich, teeming with frantic sawyers and unidentifiable debris. Cleaning the chicken house one day, I used a scoop shovel to scrape up droppings and dirtied oat hay. I shooed the squabbling hens, a new batch of chicks, and the irascible rooster outside in the sunshine. The dark air hung heavy and lung-burning, tinged with ammonia. I was in a hurry, and my shovel came down hard on a fluff-ball chick that had scurried back inside. Cheeping loudly, she dragged a broken toothpick leg. I picked her up and carried her to the cabin cupped in my hands. Bill was playing the piano, Rachmaninoff, something bold and brilliant. I dared not interrupt, so I simply held the chick out, her leg dangling. Without pausing, he said bluntly, "You hurt it. You take care of it." Afraid and crying, I asked, "Why are you so cruel?"

"Cruelty counts," he said.

Taking the peeping bird outside, I placed her on the chopping block and reached for the double-bitted ax. I put her tiny body and severed head into a matchbox and placed the makeshift coffin on a pile of slash waiting to be burned. Cremation would be a more honorable fate than being thrown to the cats or ravens. Squatting on the riverbank, I scrubbed my hands in water running with ice and cried. How could I tell Bill how deeply disturbed I felt by his dismissal of the chick's life, how difficult it was for me to close my heart to something suffering?

I assumed that death came easy for Bill. He lived as a hunter and trapper. He had served as a medic in the war. Remote and mostly silent, he considered his life hard-won. His outlook stayed stuck in a soldier's narrow vision, fierce and intent. He carried his aloneness like a shield, and his callous disregard of others gave him a separate peace. I admired and respected him, and in my own young, untaught way, I loved him. I yearned for his strength, his conviction, and his courage. Ignorant and innocent, I suffered in his realm, but I learned of many things: things of darkness and despair, things of joy and light, things of the land and the wild ones who walked there. I learned of the seasons and the value of food and shelter. Cold and fear took their place alongside laughter and warmth. I learned the incredible power of a single kerosene lamp burning at the window on the nights he did not come home. I learned to be alone.

∽

The second spring came early. The snow line retreated each day and left miniature, majestic lakes on the meadow. Wild swans glided in late in the evening; they came for last summer's seeds, and their calls sounded dusk-soft, eternal. The crazy cries of loons echoed back and forth across the land, drifting high, lonesome, and eerie in the night skies.

I had learned to ride bareback. We went one day, late in the afternoon, to see the country opening up. Bill rode the sorrel mare, Jubilee, and I, her three-year-old bay colt, Ahkee. Since the night of my botched knot-tying incident, Ahkee and I had learned to trust each other. Bill and I left the sheltered timber surrounding the cabin and barn and headed cross-country along the edge of the snow-free meadow, winding our way through willow-choked beaver sloughs, headed for higher ground. Suddenly I was cold and afraid. But Bill went on and I followed. The beaver channel of black water and ice and mud stretched wide and bottomless, and the mare lunged in and splashed and sprang ahead, scrambling for footing on the steep, slippery bank. Ahkee was young and uncertain. He minced and backed up, shying; then he plunged in after his dam, lurched, drew up in an explosion of fear, leapt the bank, crashed through the dog-hair pine, and was still. Terrified and still. He would not move. I kicked and beat him with the reins. Releasing my death grip on his mane, I slid off on jellied legs to lead him forward, but he would not move. Finally, desperately, I whooped a comeback call to Bill, who had disappeared downriver.

We could find nothing wrong. No blood; no broken bones. Nothing but that the colt was wild-eyed and trembling, coated with icy sweat. He would not move, no matter how we coaxed and cajoled. So Bill took off his hackamore and turned him loose, assuming he would follow or turn back for the barn. We rode off double on the mare, crossing the wide, roaring river channels, making our circle for home in the day's last silk-soft air.

Bill dropped me at the cabin door and raced away on the trail we had first taken. I waited and worried, sitting on the

wood block while the goats and cats gathered around and the
sunlight faded into pink and orange shimmers on the distant
snowcapped peaks. The thunder of hooves scattered the goats
and brought me to my feet as the mare slid to a stop, all foam
and frantic dancing.

"Get me the .30-.30," he said.

And I did. And he was gone.

I started a fire and lit the lamp. I half held my breath waiting
until the sharp crack of the rifle told me Ahkee was dead and I
did not know why. And I was frightened.

With caution, I stepped out into the moonlight. I took the
clammy, heavy rifle and held Jubilee's head. Bill's cheeks were
silver-streaked with tears, the first I had ever seen him cry, but
his face was horrible to see so I looked away, ashamed, and hid
my face on the mare's hot, sweat-stained neck. Then Bill was
gone to the river, down under the dark bank where the water
ran glacial and pure.

Later, we did not sleep. The moon burned bright as day, and
the upstairs room filled with an unearthly dance of light and
drifting shadows. For a long time he would not speak, and I lay
very still and scared until his tense voice, harsh and choked,
said, "A beaver stob poked a hole in his gut, and he trailed his
intestines for a quarter-mile and tromped them in the mud.
And he was down."

I could think of nothing to say; not one thing for comfort,
nothing to take away the loss of his hand-raised colt, gentle-
broke and trusting. And I never knew for many years if I was
to blame.

Death became easier for me, though it was never easy. I
began to see that everything I did had a reason, and that every
day of my life was precarious and delicate, hanging in balance.

In the Company of Rivers

After coming west, I lived in the company of rivers and creeks, and I learned to know them well. I knew the temperament of wild waters in every season of the year because I canoed on lakes and rivers, fished in tributaries, bathed and washed clothes in streams, and hauled water for drinking and cooking. Every source of water, from bare trickle to glacial freshet, influenced my life, yet none had such an impact on me as the Northfork of the Flathead. The Northfork, my first river, like a first lover, indelibly marked the girl I was and helped shape the woman I would become.

Newly separated from the crowded suburbs of Chicago, I had never had an opportunity to be around rivers, especially rivers that were wild enough, pure enough, to drink from and bathe in. From my initial encounter with the Northfork, when Bill asked me to bring up a five-gallon bucket of drinking water from the river, I knew that my relationship with the roiling, ice-choked water would be difficult. I was afraid as I tiptoed out on a slick three-inch-thick plank to reach a stretch of water deep enough to dip the bucket. The river looked mean-hearted and unforgiving. Perhaps I judged it prematurely, without even knowing anything about its personality.

Old and cold, it had a voice like a razor scraping dry skin. The river's face, seized into a permanent frown, had been sculpted out of huge ice floes and dirt-pocked snow. I had the sneaking suspicion that the Northfork would willingly swallow me alive if I happened to slip into the rushing current. For months I grudgingly visited twice a day, hauling water at dawn and at dusk. On laundry days I scrambled up the steep bank at least a dozen times to carry water for the washtubs on the wood stove, and then I lugged baskets of wet clothes down to the gelid gush, leaning out from the precarious plank to rinse and wring garments before hanging them on the clothesline to freeze-dry. My hands cracked and bled, turned a permanent beet red from dealing with the river's frigid demeanor.

As winter melted into spring, the river softened. At night its voice changed to that of a siren, coaxing me outside to listen as coyotes lined up under the budding cottonwoods to chortle. At dawn the trill of the water ouzel joined in the river's song, until they created a melody of such intense pleasure that Bill often woke me at first light to hear the "nightingale of the Rockies and the symphony of watery strings." I started to savor my moments of solitude on the secure plank, but still I gazed into the river's growing flow like a frightened child who goes kicking and screaming into the bathtub.

When runoff started, the Northfork howled, the banks crumbling beneath the intense pressure of too much water. Strange things showed up in the current: dead animals, bushes, giant uprooted trees, pieces of roofing, boards, an inner tube that bobbed and bounced as if suspended on a string from the sky. And mud, tons of mud, mud so thick the water churned cowboy-coffee brown, and it took hours for the silt to settle enough that we could drink from the bucket. During the day, the roar of the river made me edgy, off-kilter. At night, the

frenzied tempo, an insane relentless beat, kept me from
sleeping.

But by late June, the Northfork had had its fun. Worn out
and weary of rushing about, the flow eased, settling into a
summer season run that complemented the complexion of a
sweeter self, reflecting back the swaying movement of branches
and leaves in an occasional still pool. Though the water remained nipple-stiffening cold, Bill often stripped down and,
wearing only his tennis shoes, waded among the boulders until
he found a place deep enough to swim. Petrified, I watched
from the sanctuary of the high bank while the current sucked
him downstream, pulled him under, then spat him back out
like a plastic toy. Strong-shouldered and fearless, he played
with the river, swimming against the current again and again,
then letting go for a raucous ride to the nearest gravel bar. He
called and called, urging me to join him. When I refused, he
mocked my timidity and tried to shame me into getting wet. It
didn't work. The Northfork was my nemesis. The river knew
about my fear, and I accepted it as a formidable rival who
would inflict intense retribution if I made even one misstep.

Bill also knew my fear—not only my fear of the river's dangerous waters, but my fear of the dark, of being alone, of the
countless mice that roamed the rafters in the cabin, of the wild
animals I knew nothing about. He knew that if I was to thrive
in that remote landscape, I would have to face each one of
those fears on my own. He knew that I would have to come to
terms with the river that ran through each of our days and sang
through every night.

Savvy enough to understand my situation, Bill increased my
connection to the river by taking me on horseback, leading me
on Jubilee across the shallow crossings until I gained enough
confidence to ride alone. I trusted his old sorrel mare and
accepted the fact that her long legs and sturdy back would keep
me safe above the water. Playfully, Bill appealed to the girl in

me and built a board swing that hung from long pieces of thick
rope looped and tied over the high branch of a cottonwood
tree. From the grass-covered bank, he pushed me harder and
harder until I hung suspended between sky and stream for one
heart-skipped second before I stooped toward earth and back
over dry ground. At first I pinched my eyes shut and screamed,
my hands white-knuckled on the rough twists of rope. Soon,
however, I pumped my legs to go higher, and threw back my
head to see the river's world upside down. Yet even with these
escapades, I refused to go in the water except to dangle my bare
feet in the chill shallows after working all day to plant the
garden.

We rode together one afternoon. Jubilee carried us double
on her bare back. Bill reined her down the Northfork through
aspen groves and thickets of jack pine. We crossed the river
innumerable times, going farther and farther away from the
cabin as the midday sun slipped lower on the horizon. Bill
stopped on a sandbar where Sage Creek poured into the river
out of Canada. He offered his forearm so I could slide down off
Jubilee, then swung his leg over and dropped to the ground.
For the longest time we sprawled in the July sun to soak up the
warmth of the rays and the latent heat hidden in the sandy
gravel beneath us. Bill rose, brushed off his buckskin pants,
vaulted onto the mare, and rode out into the river. He left me
in shocked silence on the bank.

I called, "Come back."

He stopped Jubilee in the hock-deep flow and hollered,
"You'll have to wade."

"I can't."

"You have no choice."

He refused to come back, and the only way for me to get
back home was to cross the river countless times.

"You goddamned son of a bitch," I screamed.

He doffed his hat, waved, and rode on.

"Wait. Bill, wait. Wait. Please. I don't know how to do this."

He swung Jubilee around and rode close enough that I could hear him shout instructions: "Take off your clothes. Put your underwear and shirt inside your pants, cinch the waist shut with your belt, tie the pant legs around your neck, put your moccasins back on, and start wading."

He rode off again. The mare splashed silver streamers of water that caught the sun and sparkled all the colors of the rainbow.

I cried like a kid, swiping snot off my nose. I stomped my feet, paced, turned circles, and finally sat down shivering with my head on my knees. From far away I heard Bill's voice echoing across the wide expanse of water. "You can do it!"

I raised my head and pushed the hair out of my eyes. He stood with Jubilee on top of a sheer bluff upriver.

His deep voice wavered above the water's roar. "Cross where I crossed. I won't let you drown."

My fingers shook. I fumbled with buttons and zipper as I undressed, stuffed my clothes in my pants, and tied them around my neck. Standing naked and chicken-skinned in the sand, I swished sand off the bottoms of my feet and put my moccasins back on. One slow step at a time, I waded into the river. I asked the Northfork for forgiveness, praying for benevolence, begging not to be taken just because I was stupid. I wanted to trust Bill, but I worried that he wouldn't be able to get to me in time if the river chose to snag my fish-belly-colored flesh and suck me under.

When I was knee-deep, the river's current pushed hard against my legs. My feet slid on the slick cobble, and I went down. My arms flew out to break my fall, but before I was barely wet, I bolted upright and scrambled for footing.

"Don't look down," Bill yelled. "Keep coming."

I waded, my arms reaching out for balance like a tightrope walker as the water sucked at my thighs. I glanced at the sun-mirrored river, the shapes of stones that shimmered underneath the surface, before my eyes returned to the far bank where Bill waited on foot, the mare ground-tied in a patch of grass and sage. I maneuvered around large rocks. Something told me to stay upstream of the small whirlpools that swirled below them. I inched my way, feeling for every step. The cold water sloshed against my upstream hip, making me gasp and laugh.

"You're half way," Bill shouted.

I heard him holler "Good girl" just as the river whipped my legs out from under me and I spiraled backward down into darkness.

I came up choking and spitting. My arms reached for air, and my feet found the gravel bottom of the hole for a fast second before it disappeared again. My eyes focused on the bank. Bill sprinted downstream. He laughed, calling out, "Swim, swim." The next time my feet found the bottom, I shoved toward shore and struck out at the little waves that lapped my face. Panicked, I gulped water in fast slurps as I flailed toward willows that whisked past. I heard Bill splashing toward me. He shouted, "Close your mouth," and then he grabbed my arm and dragged me backward into the shallows.

Pissed off, I slapped at him. My wet clothes flapped against my back as I stumbled in the rocks.

"Stop," he said, trying to pin my arms. "Stop. You did it! You did it!"

I realized that I had been baptized. I had made it to the opposite shore. The Northfork had initiated me into the company of rivers. I started laughing and could not stop. Blue-lipped, I shivered hard from the hypothermic cold. Bill, wet from the waist down, whacked me on the butt and said, "Run, it will warm you up." I swung a half-hearted punch at his head, but he dodged and bolted. Laughing and crying at the same time, I pulled the wet clothes over my head, flopped them on the ground, and chased him around the pebbled bar as Jubilee watched wide-eyed from the bank.

Never again was I afraid of the Northfork. A difficult lover, moody and uncertain, fickle and ever-changing, the river never stayed the same. Every day its spirit shifted with the weather, with the seasons, with the ways in which man altered its natural composition with development, timbering, and coal mining upstream. I accepted a job with the Department of the Interior to monitor the quality of the water in our remote location. Whenever I dipped a sample bottle into the stream, I asked permission. I asked, "How are you? Holding up okay? Are you afraid of dying?" The Northfork never gave me any answer. The river continued to sing, as always, changing course whenever the weather shifted, marking the banks with whatever wonder seemed appropriate at the time.

Of Mice and Madness

When I came west, I had never seen a mouse in the flesh. The first time I saw Kriega the barn cat disemboweling a mouse on the milking stanchion, I almost threw up. When a mouse ran across my bare feet in the middle of the night, I screamed as if I were being strangled. During the long hours of darkness I lay awake, my eyes wide, staring into the cold blackness, listening to scurries and scratches and squeaks. "It's only mice," Bill said. "They're having their winter Olympics."

Bill, a veteran of both war and wilderness, found my fear of rodents so fascinating that he made it his mission to investigate the limits of my fright. He took his in-house trap line as seriously as he did the one that wound through the woods set for ermine, mink, marten, coyote, and wolverine. He baited the little wooden traps with bits of Tillamook cheese every night. Then, each morning, he sacrificed his captured carrion to the hungry cats that waited on the woodpile. Surreptitiously, he began a campaign to cure my fear. He left a dead mouse dangling on a string above the wood stove so I met it eye to eye

when I lit the fire in dawn's dim light. He left a dead mouse on
the roll of toilet tissue next to my side of the bed, so instead of
finding surcease for my runny nose, I found a stiffened lump
of fur and whiskers. It was not long before I realized that my
screaming hysterics were immeasurably entertaining to a man
who lived in an environment with no television, no visitors,
and no nights out on the town.

To prove I was tough enough to stay in his mountain hideaway, I stopped screaming and volunteered to take over the in-
house traps. Bill beamed with pleasure when I proudly brought
him my first dead mouse. He taught me how to skin the wee
carcass, take the thin membrane of flesh off the downy hide,
remove the mouse's minuscule brain, mix it with water into a
paste to use as a tanning agent, then soften the skin. In the end,
I had a mouse finger puppet, complete with eyeholes, nose,
and whiskers, with which I teased the cats. I even talked to my
mouse toy like a girl child talks to a handmade doll.

"Trespass and you are a goner" became my tough and terrible mouse credo. I became adept at killing mice whenever they
invaded my domain. It was a classic case of kill or be overrun.
Despite the fact that I had worked hard all of my adult life to
be without bias, to never judge according to ethnic origin, race,
religion, creed, or specific species, I admitted outright that I
hated mice. They left small black calling cards in the silverware
drawer, made nests in linen closets, chewed through boxes and
bags, stole food, danced in the flour bin, and kept me awake at
night. I never saw their ghostly presences, but I heard solemn
scratching and chewing. When the wind blew hard out of the
west, dark droppings drifted down to decorate the bed. I set
traps outside on the windowsills and continued to engage in a
conflict settled only by death. I had my usual morning tête-
à-têtes with foreign field mice that I enticed to meet their
maker with peanut-butter bait. I used distasteful tactics at
times and became an accomplished assassin. My kills were
quick and clean. On the rare occasion when I caught a mouse

that lived, I sent him or her to mouse heaven in a bucket of warm water. As they drowned, I prayed the prayer of all harried rural housewives: "Please, God, tell Mickey and Minnie to have their babies in someone else's house."

Still the mice made merry in my midst. With increased surveillance, I figured out that if I set traps in certain spots, I could prevent migration to the whole cabin. I abhorred the beasties. I hated setting traps and flinging corpses out the door. Yet after so many months of near-madness, I grew into a reluctant acceptance of mice in my life.

Once, after bathing, I reached under the sink for a bottle of hand lotion and found another victim squashed in death. Without a thought, without a worry, I walked outside with nothing on except a towel wound around my wet hair, dangling the mouse by its tail.

"What in the world are you doing?" Bill said.

"Nothing," I replied. "Just think of me as a new work of art—Godiva with mouse."

Later, while standing by the kitchen door, I saw a mouse meander across the counter on the porch where the cats ate. Miss Mouse walked right into the porcelain dish and helped herself. With immaculate dignity, she washed her face, combed her whiskers, and investigated the cats' beds. Then she cozied up on the windowsill for a brief nap in the sun. What pluck! What panache! She—for it had to be a she instead of a he—had huge brown eyes set in a small face, with delicate, transparent ears and silver-thread whiskers that were nearly as long as her dove-gray body. When she sat up on her pinky-tan hind legs, balanced by a graceful tail, she revealed a silken bib of white hair on her chest. Her tiny paws sported long, sharp claws, and she moved like a ballet dancer *en pointe.* I envied her courage. I wished for her nonchalant bravery.

The mother superior of cats exited the shed and headed across the yard. Miss Mouse, oblivious to impending disaster, nibbled a star-shaped piece of cat food. I swallowed as I made

one of life's difficult decisions. I tapped lightly on the door's
frame and pointed outside. Miss Mouse raised her head,
looked at me, looked at the cat, and ducked into the woodpile.

∾

If mice were bad, rats were worse. Not only did pack rats invade
any available space found within the confines of the Northfork
homestead, they left their rancid odor and slimy scent trails.
They stole things, especially anything shiny, like bullet casings
and pieces of tin foil. When a rat found its way into the cabin,
Bill declared war. He had a foolproof rattrap: a coffee can with
an ought trap set inside baited with a dried plum. Rats could
not resist. They dove into the can headfirst and were caught. In
most cases, the tight-springed trap killed them outright. In
some cases, further molestation was required to get rid of the
creatures. Despite their rank musk, pack rats sport silky fur and
long, fuzzy tails. This made them more endearing than the city
rats with their naked pink, scaly tails. And their pelts, along with
those of the excess kittens, became warm backings for mittens.

When a rat began devouring the grain in the barn, Bill set a
trap in the top of the feed barrel with specific instructions: Use
care in case the rat got caught only by a foot. Do not try to grab
it. Club it with a stick or get the .22. When I went out to do
chores the next morning, there was something in the trap.
Only it was not a rat. It was a white cat we called Deaf Smith.
He yowled and held up his trap-bound front paw. Forgetting
that an injured cat still has twenty claws, I rushed to his aid. He
proceeded to scratch the hell out of my arms, chest, and throat.
Bleeding and cussing, I walked back to the cabin to get Bill. He
came back with me, threw a burlap sack over the cat, and then,
while I held the terrified feline down, Bill extracted his paw
from the metal jaws. Poor Deaf Smith hobbled around on a
swollen stump for a week, but he eventually healed.

The rats liked to enter the cabin at a favorite spot. Between
the main roof and the summer kitchen wall, there lay a hidden

entrance that was impossible to seal shut. With the trap chain nailed to the wall, Bill kept a trap set there. He told me to check the trap every morning and night, and if we caught a rat, to shoot it with the .22. Then he went to town.

The first night Bill was gone, a horrendous clanging and clawing came from the cabin roof. I jumped out of bed, the growling dog at my heels, grabbed a flashlight, and discovered a rat. A big rat—suspended by the trap and chain—flopped and fought in the dark. With no way to hold a light and a rifle at the same time, I curled up on the couch and plugged my ears with cotton to keep from hearing the racket. Come dawn, the rat was still there and still very much alive. The pathetic thing with beady black eyes and amazingly long whiskers stared at me. As soon as there was enough light to see, I braced the .22 against the cabin's log frame, took aim, and missed. Not once, but many times. Little brass casings piled up at my feet. No matter how I adjusted the rifle, I could not hit the rat. I only enraged the exhausted creature, made myself feel sick, and upset the dog, cats, horses, goats, rabbits, and chickens.

I dragged the ladder out from the shed, propped it against the side of the logs, got a piece of stove wood, and climbed up to do battle. It took me several tries to nail the rat while clinging precariously to the ladder. When he hung limp, I said a prayer of gratitude with great relief. I tossed the dead rat to the dog. She proceeded to maul it, throw it in the air, and grab it again on the downfall. She flung it side to side in her mouth as if to kill an already dead creature. She barked at it, trying to get the beast to wake up and play. I did not reset the trap.

For years I fought an all-out, never-ending war with rats in barns, sheds, granaries, furnace vents, vehicle engines, and woodpiles. Despite my environmental ethic to love all things of the natural world, I never found a way to accept rats. My mom schooled me from a very young age never to say "I hate," but I hated rats. I hated rats. I hated rats. I still hate rats.

Trap Trail

As with everything else, Bill started me out small with my lessons in trapping. Though mice came first, I graduated to trapping pack rats in the winter and shooting ground squirrels in the summer. The white tomcat, Kriega, helped me skin the critters. He blissfully gnawed on a haunch as I worked the tip of my knife against the pale, stretchy fibers that held fur to muscle. Working around the ears and eyes was the most delicate part of the art, and it took me a long while to master enough patience to pull off a flawless case-skinned pelt. Mixing the brains with warm water to tan the hides proved a complicated process.

By my second winter, I was expert enough to try my hand at real furs. My first victim was an ermine that got caught in the trap we had set near the chicken coop at night after the birds had sought their roosts. Something had stolen a hen every second or third night. Bill correctly suspected a weasel. When I went out at dawn with a hot kettle to thaw out the chickens' water dish, I found the long, snow-white body with the black-tipped tail. With a deftness acquired from my mouse and rat

days, I opened the trap, removed the ermine, held it in one
hand while I dished out scratch for the chickens, then walked
back to the cabin. Thinking the creature dead, I plopped it
down on the kitchen table to refill the kettle and get breakfast
started. The warm room brought the ermine back to life, and
my first recognition of its reincarnation was Kriega making a
flying leap from his bed on the chair after a white airborne
streak. For a couple of moments, the cabin turned into chaos
as cat chased weasel up and down, round and round. My first
thought was that I didn't want Bill to find out how dumb I had
been. My second thought was to get the thing out of the house
before it tore into the cat or bit me. Yet I didn't dare let the
beast go free for fear that it would go right back to killing
chickens. I slipped out and closed the woodshed door, flung
open the cabin door, raced around the stove to herd both racing white forms out, then slammed the door and picked up a
thick piece of kindling to use as a club. Kriega beat me. He
snagged the ermine in front of me on the woodshed floor, and I
promptly stepped on it. Bill walked in and saved me from having to dispatch the weasel. He looked at me with an odd grin,
and I said, "Kriega got it." Bill bent over, grabbed the ermine by
the throat, snapped its neck, and laid the body on top of the
dog's house just inside the door. "Nice one," he said. "Do you
want to skin and tan it?"

After that, Bill trusted my ability. He took me with him on
snowshoes to check beaver traps and showed me how to dip a
willow into the castor scent and place the withe just right. He
taught me how to rig the trap so when the metal jaws clamped
shut, the beaver would dive and drown, an easier death than
freezing. I didn't understand the dying part or why Bill felt it
necessary to trap. Wouldn't we be kinder if we allowed the beaver and other fur-bearers the right to live their lives in peace?
He explained that he took only a few pelts a year, monitoring
with care the places where the animals lived, how many were in
the territory, and when they were overpopulated. Nature had

her way of preventing some of that with predators and diseases like tularemia, but he was convinced that what he took helped achieve a fair balance. The furs he tanned were never sold. He kept them and turned them into coats, vests, mittens, and hats for his own use against the day when the government over-stepped its bounds, the people revolted, society collapsed, and the world turned to mayhem. After the horrors of Vietnam, Bill remained convinced of the inevitable demise of the world as we knew it. Determined to be prepared, he lived the old ways, with no dependence on electricity, manufactured goods like clothes and shoes, or processed foods. Though I did not want to believe in Armageddon, he had a point. His other point, strongly enforced, was that if I wanted to remain in his world, then I needed to learn the skills to provide for and pro-tect myself in the event that he did not come home one day. That meant becoming competent with a pistol, rifle, knife, bow, tomahawk, saw, ax, and traps.

I wore a pack board on the beaver runs, and when we had more than one beaver to bring home, I carried the round, blubbery beasts on my back, their monkey-like paws waving as I walked. Bill taught me how to skin and flesh the hides and stitch them into round willow frames to dry, scrape, and then braintan. We ate the meat and the fatty tails, but when there was more than enough, we fed the flesh to the dogs, cats, and chickens. Or we put the carcasses up on the roofs for the mag-pies and ravens. We kept the front paws, dried them, sewed buckskin caps on top with beadwork, and made ornaments to honor the beaver. We saved the long teeth for necklaces and the back toes to use as buttons. Nothing went to waste. Bill spent many long winter hours carefully pulling the long, stiff guard hairs from the tanned plews, leaving behind only the soft underfur, which made the pelt perfect for sleeping on.

When the road snowed shut (and word was that the county would not be plowing farther than Trail Creek, and neither would the private logging company that sometimes kept the

track open to the border), Bill set traps for pine marten
and ermine along the four-mile-long trail that we snowshoed
to retrieve the mail. Sometimes he traveled alone; sometimes
we went together. One time I headed out by myself, with
instructions on what to do if I found something in a trap.
I had watched Bill often enough that I knew the stun-and-
strangle process and wasn't afraid to go alone. "If you find a
wolverine caught by a toe," he said as I buckled on my snowshoes, "come and get me."

He had told me the story of trapping a wolverine, of the
ensuing snarling and snapping battle before he waded in once
again and struck a good blow with a broken ax handle. Bill had
not intended to catch a wolverine; they were rare. He had set
the trap for coyote, but when he found the skunk bear caught
with a damaged foot, he had no way of releasing it back into
the wild. Thinking it dead, he put the carcass in his backpack
and headed downcountry to show our closest neighbor, Old
Tom Reynolds. No sooner had Bill arrived at the cabin to call
Old Tom outside to see the wolverine than he felt the animal
stirring on his back. Knowing he had only stunned the beast
and not hit it hard enough to kill it, Bill whipped off his pack,
dumped the snarling thing onto the snow, clipped it in the
head again, and then strangled it in front of Old Tom, all without saying a word. I wasn't sure I believed this tale, so one time
when I was alone with Old Tom, I came right out and asked
him. He verified the story, saying, "I'd never seen a man look so
scared or move so fast in my life. I thought he had planned the
whole thing for my personal entertainment. After he had made
certain the thing was dead and caught his breath and told me
the whole story, I laughed until I was sick."

At the first three sets, I found nothing but frozen pine squirrels, which I put in my pack to take home for the cats. At the
fourth set, I spotted movement through the trees and stopped.
Taking off my pack and my snowshoes, I searched for and
found a short, stout stick and inched forward. Not a squirrel,

but a marten caught by a hind leg. He had smelled me and now stood clinging to the branch of the pine, his black eyes glossy and sharp, his lips pulled back to expose his small, sharp teeth. I thought of walking away, of telling Bill that I had found nothing in the traps. Then I thought of the marten, which I knew would struggle for hours until the night cold froze the breath in his lungs. If I hesitated one more second, I would be in tears. Dashing forward, I swung the stick and missed. The marten leapt, hissing and screaming. He dangled for a moment from the trap's chain, grabbed the tree, and positioned his body again for my attack. This time I did not miss. When he swung lifeless, I took off my mittens and pried open the trap, while stomping a flat place in the snow. When he was free, I grabbed him around the neck with one fist and around the middle of his body with the other. His heart still beat, the small pounding against my palm burning hot. Still keeping my chokehold, I bent and put him on the tromped ground and stepped on his rib cage, pushing all the air from his lungs. I stayed that way until the ravens came to caw out their warnings, and I knew he was dead.

I placed his limp body over a branch and smoothed his fur. Then I reset the trap, put on my pack, strapped on my snowshoes, and picked him up. Remembering Bill's dead-but-alive wolverine story, I did not want to put the marten in my pack, so I carried him in my left hand, my fingers gripped around his throat. My right hand carried my ski pole, but I had had enough sense to save the stout stick and had it stuck in my belt next to my knife. All was well until I felt the fleas leave the marten's chilling body and begin an ascent up my arm. I threw the carcass to the ground and stepped on it with my snowshoe and flicked off the fleas. Surely the marten was dead if the vermin were searching for another warm body. I picked him up by his fine fluffy tail, and with him dangling there at arm's length, I made my way around the corner of the road to Old Tom's mailbox. I still had three miles to Trail Creek and four miles home. It would be easier to put the marten in a safe place while I traveled. Without thinking further, I curled him in a circle in the dark confines and closed the box's lid. I would be picking up Old Tom's mail, too, so when I got back I could make the exchange, giving him his letters and bills and retrieving the marten to take home to Bill.

I strolled on, tapping my ski poke against my snowshoes every few steps to dislodge the clobbered snow sticking to the shellacked rawhide. I began to worry about Old Tom and the marten. What if Old Tom snowshoed down off his mountain and opened his mailbox? What if the marten was not really dead? What if a snarling fury leapt out and nailed him in the face? He wouldn't think it funny, and neither would I. I picked up my pace.

At the last trap set, I was surprised to see a flush of red all over the snow leading toward the tree. It had melted into the white, leaving a ghastly smear. It couldn't be blood, or could it? I stood a long while listening and heard nothing but the wind and the far-off calling of the gray jays that Bill called camp robbers. I watched, but saw no movement in the vicinity. Finally I walked forward, and there, nailed to the tree, was a notice written with black marker on a brown paper bag: "Murderer. Vicious fiend. Despicable slaughterer of innocent animals. Stay away."

Sweat sprang out all over my body, and the hair on my arms and neck stiffened. The trap had been sprung with a rock, and the red whatever had been splashed on the tree and trickled all over the area. I backed up, not taking my eyes off the note. I had no idea if the upset person lurked nearby, or if the angry words had been penned days ago. I felt for my stick, for my knife, then felt foolish. It was one thing to clobber a small pine marten; it was another to take on a full-grown crazy person. I stopped again and listened and heard nothing. Even the jays had gone quiet. Then I turned and ran, spraddle-legged on my snowshoes, back out to the main trail on the road. The mailboxes at Trail Creek were no more than a quarter-mile away. I had to get the mail and then get home.

By the time I had jog-shuffled back to Old Tom's mailbox, left his few letters, and picked up the marten, still curled nose to tail, and stuffed it in my pack, I was exhausted. I plodded the last miles toward home, the triumph of my kill distorted and ruined by the crazy person's crucified missive. There were so few people in the valley. Was it someone we knew? Or a visitor? What would Bill do? Should I even tell him? Knowing Bill, would he go and reset the fouled trap and then lie in wait with his rifle cradled on his knees to see who came back to check?

Raising Rabbits

Coming in from running the trap trail, I tried to fake some exuberance when I shuffled up to the cabin door with my hips burned out and my heels blistered. The hound came out to sniff at the pack I dropped at my feet. Bill stood in the doorway eating a yellow delicious apple he had brought up from the root cellar. "How did you do?" he asked.

"I brought back some squirrels for the cats and reset the traps," I said.

"Any problems?" he asked.

"Just this," I said, and pulled out the marten to hand him.

"Good girl. He's beautiful. I'll help you tan him so the fur won't slip."

I told him about the marauding fleas and putting the marten in Old Tom's mailbox. He laughed, stroking the rich dark fur.

"When you get enough pelts," he said, "we'll make you a vest or a jacket."

"I can't go for the mail anymore," I said.

"What?" he asked.

I spoke up. "I can't go for the mail anymore. I can't run the traps."

"Why not?" he asked. "You did just fine."

I tried not to cry, but the words came bubbling out through choked sobs and the snot running from my nose, which I tried without success to wipe away with shaking hands. Bill listened to what I said about the note and the red snow. He took his snowshoes down from the wall and set them side by side in the fresh drift beyond the snowless flagstones in front of the door. Then he turned and went back into the cabin for his boots and coat.

When he returned, he strapped his wide belt with the hand-forged knife around his waist and tucked in his small tomahawk. He had not brought out a rifle.

"Bill?" I scratched the hound's head.

"Don't worry," he said. "I think I know who it is. I'm not going to track him down. I'm just going to go pull the traps. We'll run a line farther north from now on. You did the right thing to tell me. I'll teach you how to use the pistol, okay? Then when you go alone, you won't have to be afraid."

"Okay," I said. "I still don't want to run the traps. I'm not tough enough to take the pain I see in their eyes."

He looked at me for a long time. Was he trying to decide whether I should be forced to leave or be allowed to stay?

"You still have rabbits and goats. Would you like a rabbit coat instead?" he asked.

"Yes."

"I'll be home before dark. If I'm not, wait until morning, then go up to Old Tom's and stay there. Okay?"

"All right."

∾

I tried to bead the otter tail I had been working on, but I was so restless and upset that I could not sit still. I wandered outside to get water, then wandered back inside to put wood on the fire. I stared at the elk and moose robes on the walls, the seven-foot-long mountain lion hide draped over a chair, the bear hide on the back of the couch, the coyotes and lynx hanging from their nostrils on the tines of the six-point elk racks. I studied the marten and mink parka, the fox hat, the beaver vest, and the stack of just-smoked deer hides folded with care. On the long table there were arrowheads and scrapers, ball-and-cap carved-handled pistols, handmade arrows and knives, a .50 caliber muzzleloader, a couple of old rusted traps. Each weapon and each animal represented miles and miles of snowshoeing or hiking and tracking or setting traps. Each represented Bill's dedication to wildness, his willingness to study untamed lives and the patterns of behavior. He had taught me not to fear the animals that walked in the wild. He had also taught me to fear the ones that walked on two legs. If I respected the four-legged creatures' natural proclivities and understood their boundaries, I had no reason to run from them, because they feared me most of all. Men were a different story. No matter how much I studied or philosophized, the human race seemed impossible to understand, to know, or to trust.

～

I was cleaning the rabbits' cages and giving them new hay when Bill returned just as dusk gave way to dark. He slung the string of wire-wrapped traps to the ground and unbuckled his snow-shoes. Clapping them together to remove the snow, he said, "I left the note where it was to remind him of his own idiocy. He won't last the winter. They never do. What's for supper?"

"Supper?" I said. I had forgotten about supper. I let the black doe sniff my fingers through the wire.

"Starshine's decided she's in love with Starbuck. How long do I have to wait before I can breed them?" I asked.

"Late spring," he said. "Any sooner and the babies will freeze. You shouldn't name them if we're going to eat them."

"I know, but I can't keep calling them both 'Bun-Bun' all the time. How many pelts will I need to make a coat?"

"About sixty or seventy if you want a long coat."

"That's a lot of rabbits," I said, filling the water dishes. "A lot of butchering."

"Yep. Let's go eat. Bring some canned meat from the root cellar."

In May, when Starshine had her first litter, she killed every one of her naked, squirming offspring. When I told Bill, he said, "Kill her."

"Don't you think she deserves another chance?" I asked.

"She'll do it again. If she doesn't have any mothering instinct now, she never will."

"I don't see why—"

"Do what you want to do," he said. "They're your rabbits. But you'd better find a way to buy feed for them if you're going to keep them as pets."

I waited a week and then gathered Starshine in my arms, whispered sweet words to her, and put her in Starbuck's cage. I watched, mesmerized, as he courted her, getting her used to his company, and then mounted and bred her with frenzied thrusts. With the honeymoon over, I put Starshine back into her own abode and began marking the days off the calendar. As I approached thirty slash marks, I watched her carefully. She tore fur from her belly and lined a hay nest. She ate more pellets and drank more water. She had a passel of babies and killed them all. I never told Bill. I hated it that he was right. I waited for an afternoon when he was away from the cabin, picked up a small piece of stove wood, and walked out to the pen with the rabbit cages.

Starshine sat in the sun, her nose twitching. I reached through the wire door, grabbed her by the scruff of the neck, and pulled her out. Her hind claws raked open the underside of my forearm. Dripping blood, I held her by her back legs and clubbed her behind the ears. The first blow didn't do the trick, but her pained scream brought the dog and cats and goats and horses running to see what was going on. I hit her again, and again, saying, "I'm sorry, I'm sorry."

When she stopped quivering, I touched her glazed staring eye to make sure she was dead. Then I gave her to the hound. I did not have the heart to gut and skin her. Her once-silky black hair had lost its luster and was matted and tangled. I didn't care about a rabbit coat. I didn't care about wasting her meat. All I cared about was being tough enough to do what I had to do.

After sloshing water on my bleeding arm, I gave Starbuck a few pellets and told him not to worry or be afraid. He wasn't next on the list. I fondled his long pink ears and said, "The next time I go to town, I'll get you a new girlfriend, one that will be a good mother."

Wasn't that the way of the world? If you didn't do your job right, if you failed to meet the demands of your prescribed role, you were clubbed or thrown to the dogs. When you were out of the way, the guy got a new girlfriend.

Getting to Town

A wet spring. The snow was gone, but the ground stayed soggy
with several days of rain. Our doe goats had freshened, and
Bill was anxious to get a buck to breed them. The road out to
Kalispell meant sixty-five miles of mud to Columbia Falls
before it turned to gravel, then pavement. We had the buck
already lined up via the mail: Bill's close friend Nancy raised
purebred goats, and that spring she planned to breed her does
to a newly purchased buck with a fresh bloodline. She volunteered to loan us her older buck, Mayo. The only problem
remained the sea of muck we had to cross to get to town.

The weather turned cold one night in May, and everything
carried a mantle of shimmering frost the following morning.
Bill rose before dawn to build fires and make tea. He wanted to
get a move on while the road was set up like concrete from the
freeze. I packed him a lunch. He chained up and gassed up the
one-ton stock truck, and then he was gone. I had to stay behind
to do the chores and bottle-feed a dozen kids.

The day disappeared as I hauled water from the river and split stove wood and kindling and cared for the animals. I spent the afternoon sitting by the window looking out at the river, which roared with the increasing runoff volume. Stitching on a piece of beadwork to occupy my hands, I kept one ear cocked for the sound of an engine. With no near neighbors and no tourist traffic this early in the season, the noise of a motor could only mean that Bill was nearly home.

An eerie dark arrived. The sky, which had boasted brilliant sun all day, drooped with heavy clouds, and the air turned oppressive. The wind kicked up. The horses and goats, sensing another storm out of Canada, paced restless circles near the barn. I fed and milked again, and tucked the kids into a hay house I had made out of old bales. The horses hung close, which was unusual; ordinarily they would be out at dusk picking around for any new bits of green grass growing up through last year's stubble.

Back at the cabin, I lit the propane lamp and carried in more wood for the night fire. Straining the milk into gallon glass jars, I took them one by one out to the root cellar to cool. I let the dog in and put the cats out. I kept reminding myself that I didn't have to worry about Bill. After a lifetime outdoors and a dozen years of mountain living, he was capable of getting himself out of any jam he might have gotten into.

By nine, my eyes ached from reading by kerosene lamplight. My ears hurt from straining to hear the truck over the sound of the river. Wind rushed through the pines. Giving up my vigil, I took off my buckskin pants and moccasins to curl up on the couch with a bear robe over me for warmth.

I woke to someone calling my name. I sat up. The fire had burned low, and the wind whined a terrible racket, accompanied by a piece of loose tin on the roof that creaked and screamed. There, again, my name being called from a long way off: Lor-eeeee . . . ooh, ooh, ooh . . . Lor-eeeee . . . ooh, ooh,

ooh. Then nothing but silence and the noise of the wind. Shivers clawed up my spine and I widened my eyes, partly in fear, partly from trying to see something besides the pale out-line of the night sky outside the uncurtained windows.

I sat listening. The goat herd thundered past. Bells clanged against a chorus of bleats and baas. I stumbled in the dark until I found the matchbox on the countertop above the cook stove. I struck one of the matches, and it flared to life. The door flew open, and the wind blew out the tiny flame. Spilling matches everywhere, I bumbled for another one.

"Bill, is that you?"

I struck the match against the cast-iron eye of the stove. Bill hovered in the door, silent as a specter, mud up to his ankles, long black hair half-escaped from his beaded headband all blown about in a fury, his beard and mustache dripping. He grinned, and laughter rumbled out of his throat. In my long johns and flannel shirt, I shook as if I had seen a ghost. The burning match singed my fingers. I flicked it aside and plunged us into darkness again.

"You silly son of a bitch," I said, "you scared me spitless!"

Bill found a match on the floor and lit the lamp overhead. I cleaned up the others and got the fire going and the kettle on. Bill told his story in bits and pieces: he had made Kalispell fine, though he needed the chains when the road softened in the sun. He had been to the feed store and made several stops to see friends, who suggested places where he could go to sell his elk antler engravings to pay for gas and buy a couple of weaner pigs. Nancy wasn't home, so he had to wait on her. They had to enjoy their long-awaited visit before he could load up the black-and-tan buck with long, white-speckled ears. The pig farmer had several shoats on hand that had leg abscesses. He was too swamped with spring work to doctor them properly, so he offered Bill two thirty-pound porkers for free just to get them off his hands. Ready to head for home, Bill worried about the warm day. He knew the road would again be a gulf of mud.

Instead of heading out, he looked up a friend to visit for a few hours. They went out to eat so the cold night air could set up the mud. Long after dark, Bill finally drove out of town with a load of hay and grain, two pigs in burlap sacks, a couple of bags of fresh fruit and vegetables, and a lonely bleating goat.

The Northfork road was fine at first, but when the gravel ran out, it worsened. Bill chained up in a misty rain. He had some serious doubts about making it home, but figured there was no place for him to stop with all the feed and animals. He would get as far as he could. Mile after mile, he wrestled the truck in granny gear as the wipers worked hard against a drizzle turned to sleet. He had just passed the Trail Creek turnoff when he fishtailed around a sharp bend, and the soft shoulder sucked the truck off into the borrow ditch. He tried several times to work his way back up onto the roadbed only to find himself mired more deeply in the muck. He gave up and started walking.

He began calling my name at Colt's Creek, where he dropped off the ridge and crossed the meadows instead of following the longer roundabout route of the road. He hoped I would hear him and get the fire going, because he needed something to eat and drink.

"I got the horses in," he said between bites of canned elk stew. "We gotta go back."

"Back where?" I asked. His eyes showed me what a dumb question I had asked.

"To the truck. I can't get it dug out tonight, so we've got to get that goat and those pigs into a dry barn. Old Mayo's all shed off from spring in the lowlands, and the pigs are too young to weather a cold night. Besides, the bears are out grubbing for groceries. I didn't give anything for the pigs, but I sure as hell hate to sacrifice them as bear bait."

The thought of pigs and bears kept me quiet.

"I put the grain and the groceries in the cab of the truck, and the rain won't hurt the half-load of hay, but we've got to get the

animals home. That means a packhorse. Bundle up—it's getting cold out."

By the time I had rinsed the dishes and dressed and stoked
the fire, Bill had Jere and his new Appaloosa stud, War Eagle,
saddled, and he had tightened the cinch on Jubilee's Decker
packsaddle. A Coleman lamp cast flickering shadows on the
barn walls. The does lay huddled in a corner chewing cuds. The
kids baaed from inside their hay house. The hound, Kyote,
paced in and out the door.

"Sorry, pooch," Bill said, closing her inside the barn, "you've
got to stay here."

The drizzle had dwindled. Despite the cold air, the sky had
not cleared. "Blacker than a stack of black cats in a well hole,"
Bill said as he hooked the lantern to a shovel blade and swung
it rifle-style over his shoulder. He swung up on the Appy. I
handed him Jubes's lead rope, then clawed onto Jere's back.
The light and shadows danced as we picked our way across the
meadow and up the timbered ridge to the road.

It was cold and unearthly quiet, with no wind. The trees that
edged the road barely stirred. I asked a question, but Bill's stern
glare said "Keep quiet." I hunched my shoulders and dug Jere
with my heels.

An Unbelievable Night

In his stock rack prison, the buck goat must have heard us coming. He bleated as if a bear were bringing him down. We gigged the horses into a trot, and the truck came into view. Mayo had his front feet on the stock rack. With just the tip of his nose showing over the tailgate, he carried on like an off-key opera singer.

"Okay," Bill yelled. "We hear you. Now shut up before you bring in every griz and coyote this side of the divide."

I tied Jere to the back of the truck and crawled in. Mayo, wet, bedraggled, and shivering, tried to maul me with affectionate shoves. His clownish white ears flopped up and down. The lantern backlit three horses tied to a stock truck, a man and a girl lifting a huge buck goat down to the ground, and a frantic search for two weaner pigs that had escaped their burlap sacks. Bill finally found the smart little buggers squirmed between bales to keep warm. When he tried to pull them out by their hind legs, they squealed. It was an ungodly sound. Frantic, the horses reared against their ropes. Mayo dragged me down the road. If I had not been so cold and tired, the whole thing might have been funny.

Getting the pigs packed on Jubilee proved a challenge. Once Bill had the porkers in the sacks, they quieted down with little grunts and sighs. He loaded one side of the Decker with a sack of dog food and the other with groceries. The rodeo began when he tried to put the twin pigs on opposite sides to balance the weight. Jubes, unhappy about having strange-smelling, weird-sounding critters on her back, crow-hopped and threw her head.

"Settle down, you goddamned old sow." Bill slapped her roughly on the butt with his rope. He grumbled in a sweet voice: "Just like a stupid mare, fussy, fussy. I've loaded out enough bull elk and bear on you to feed an army, and you act all squeamish about a couple of little old pigs."

I imagined Jubes's unspoken response: "Sure, you old grouch, but those elk and bear were dead, and these damned things are alive and squirming and squealing."

Finally we were ready to head home. The horses had calmed. I was on Jere with Jubes's lead rope in hand. She was still snorting and tossing her head, but she tried to behave like a well-mannered lady. Bill had hooked his lariat to Mayo's collar to lead him like a horse. Little did he know that Master Mayo wasn't broke to lead. Bill cussed and cajoled. He begged and pleaded. He talked nonsense and then threatened immediate death. But Mayo planted his feet and would not budge.

Bill's patience lasted five minutes. He lost it and jabbed the Appy in the guts with his heels for an all-out pull. Mayo slid up the road, all four feet stuck out straight, his neck stretched like a rubber band.

"Stop. Bill, stop. You're choking him."

When the rope loosened, Mayo fell to his knees wheezing, his eyes bulging and his mouth gaped open like a fish out of water.

"Okay," Bill said. "One more time, calmly."

He eased his horse forward until the rope tightened, but Mayo would not move. Bill tried again, to no avail. He attempted to coax the buck one step at a time, and it was still no go. The drama repeated like a bad scene in a western. Bill threw down his rope, dismounted, and tied the lariat around Mayo's body. He remounted and started forward. Mayo balked again.

"Huh!" Bill yelled and goosed his horse into an all-out gallop. Mayo didn't even try to keep his feet. He collapsed, bleating, and let himself be dragged on his side in the mud.

"Stop! You're gonna kill him."

A supreme shouting match developed. The scene: a man and a girl screaming at each other in the middle of the night on a dark, deserted road with a stud, a mare, a gelding, two weaner pigs, and a roughed-up billy goat for an audience.

"You can't do this. He isn't even ours. He's just on loan. He's a purebred with a pedigree, worth several thousand dollars that we don't have. If you kill him or injure him, how will we pay Nancy?"

When I mentioned Nancy's name, Bill stopped yelling. The silence stabbed worse than the yelling. I thought I had committed the ultimate sin. He said, "You know, she told me something strange. She said if I ever had to lead him, to just grab on to one of his ears and he would follow me anywhere."

I looked at Bill, then at Mayo. No way. That goat was as stubborn as a jack mule, and he wasn't going to do anything that he didn't want to do.

"Here," Bill said, "hold my horse."

He untied Mayo, then coiled his rope and tied it to his saddle. He squatted down on his haunches beside the goat, who looked like he had been on a bender.

"Okay, Mayo, my boy, we'll do it your way," Bill said. He rubbed Mayo's head and scratched him on the knobby stubs where his horns had been burned off. He took hold of one of Mayo's long, droopy, white-speckled ears and said, "Let's go home." Away they went. Bill laughed as Mayo marched daintily by his side.

I shook my head. A six-foot-tall mountain man leading a muddy, prancing billy goat by his ear down a road in the middle of nowhere.

The mare nickered as they disappeared in the dark. I climbed on Jere, switched the lead ropes for the mare and stud into my right hand, and urged us all into a trot to catch up.

"Head on home," Bill said. "I'll be along as fast as Mayo's tiny feet will carry him."

"How's he behaving?" I asked.

"Fine. Just like a gentleman. He likes me to sing to him."

I rode on, leading two horses. Bill's melodic voice sang: "Boots and Stetson and six-guns and the lilies grow high. They grow for a man with a gunslingin' hand who before his time must die—must dieeeeeeeeeeeeeeeeee."

For a change, the stud behaved himself and did not try to take a hunk out of Jere. Jubilee forgot she had two pigs on her back. I made good time and kept the horses at a fast walk or a slow jog. As I crossed the Colt's Creek bridge and headed up the other side of the draw, Jubilee reared, nearly pulling me out of the saddle. I shouted "Whoa" as I tried to hang on to the ropes and reins and grab leather all at once.

Jubilee ducked her head to buck. I let go of the crazed stud. He thundered up the road toward home. Jere spooked and tried to run as well. My hands full with the rodeo mare, I jerked Jere to a stop. I jumped clear but lost control of his reins. He whirled and galloped full-bore after the Appy. I gripped the mare's lead rope with both hands and tried to talk her out of her fit.

"Whoa, girl," I said over and over. "Whoa, now, honey. Okay. Okay. What's wrong?"

I inched my way up the rope, and she quit struggling. The pigs quieted down. Poor Jubes shook all over and broke into a cold sweat. Her eyes rolled wild and white in the dark, and her ears were laid back tight. I brushed my hand along her neck and felt my way back to the Decker. The saddle wasn't there. I couldn't see a thing, but I could sure as hell tell there was no saddle on her back. I still heard the pigs grunting and rustling, so I knew they were close by. I knelt and felt the saddle, pigs and all, twisted halfway under her heaving belly. Here we were: an old mare nuts with fear, a frightened girl, a stud and a gelding racing in the night, the silence broken only by the thudding of hearts and the whisper of the creek far below.

I waited until Jubilee calmed enough to stand still. I tried to right the saddle, since there was no way to lead her the way it was. I needed both hands for the saddle, so I tied her lead rope to my belt. Every time I moved the saddle, the pigs squealed or grunted and Jubes jerked back. I couldn't get the tight cinch loose, nor could I turn the heavy saddle. Even if I got the saddle off, which meant finagling the breast collar and the britchin' strap on her rump, I knew I couldn't lift it back on the mare without unloading the pigs and the groceries and repacking everything. There was no way I was going to risk losing the weaners in the night with bears lurking.

The only thing I could do was wait. So I did. I tried not to think of Bill's reaction when he found me in the road with two horses missing. I listened for any hint of his coming in the double-black night.

The click of hooves on the wood bridge sounded, and I heard Bill say, "Almost home, Mayo, me boy, almost home."

"Bill, is that you?"

"Now who else would it be? What's wrong now?"

"The mare," I said. "The pigs. Jere and Eagle ran off. I didn't know what to do. The saddle. The pigs."

"You sound like an incompetent idiot," he said coming up alongside me. "Here, hold on to Mayo. Are the pigs still in the pack?"

"Yes. It slid under her belly," I whispered.

I held Jubes's head, chanting "Whoa" while Bill heaved the saddle upright and adjusted the pads, telling the pigs in no uncertain terms to shut up or they would be bacon much sooner than planned. He re-cinched the Decker, then straightened out the britchin' under Jubes's tail and patted her on the neck. He gave me a quick uncommon hug.

"No harm done," he said. "Only a mile to go. Let's go."

We found the horses, trailing their ropes and reins, grazing on the meadow. We led them home as well. After sticking Mayo in a stall and wiring the gate so he wouldn't escape to be with the does, we unsaddled in silence. We put the pigs in another stall with a foot of dry loose hay for bedding, then turned the horses out to roll. Walking back to the cabin carrying the groceries, we said nothing. The sleepy hound trailed our heels.

Bill agreed to let me cuddle close in bed. Everything still felt surreal: the day's bizarre events, the fact that we had not encountered any bears, the blessing that the animals were safe in the barn, the confusing circumstance of Bill's encouraging me to stay and sleep with him. One moment he raged, the next he calmed. He either shunned me or embraced me. How was I ever going to figure out such a complicated man? How was I ever going to measure up to his expectations? The clouds drifted a little, and the moon peeked out to send a signal through the open window. For once, all seemed well at the end of an unbelievable night.

Raising Goats

The goats bleated and raised a chorus to tell me it was late.
When I didn't come at once to milk and feed them, they
trooped to the cabin door and stood in semicircle formation,
calling again. Buckets in hand, I was besieged on the way to
the barn by a crowd of running hooves and pushing heads.
Everyone—goats, dog, cats, and hog—fought to push through
the low door at once, so I waited a moment on the threshold
and sniffed the spring earth and hay and animal droppings.
I tossed hay and scolded, "Kimi, get back. Come here, little
Klaire, here's your share." During the ruckus, the older goats
butted and shoved. I heard one wee voice crying outside. I went
to the door and leaned against the log frame. Two-week-old
Kandita was lost, running in circles, calling for the rest of
the herd.

"Come on, baby," I sang to her, "everyone else is inside."

She pranced up, leapt once to clear the high doorsill, and
sprawled backward to the ground. Laughing, I lifted her over
the obstacle and made room for her at the manger.

Hunched over the stanchion, pulling warm, firm teats, I listened to the hiss of milk in the bucket and the morning song of the robins. I collected my buckets as the herd wandered outside to doze in the early sun. The does flagged their tails in contentment, chewing cuds and grunting with delight. The kids ran elated circles, leaping, bucking, kicking up miniature hooves, and butting heads in mock battle. I left them all in the sunshine and carried the milk to the cabin, the cats mewing at my heels.

The Northfork goats became my substitute family and friends. I found them intelligent company because they listened politely and seldom gave me any backtalk. Best of all, they never criticized me or made me feel unworthy. In contrast, because I was the one who tended to their needs, they adored me and needed me. For a quiet, fearful girl who had grown up nearly invisible in a family of talkers and arguers, I found sweet kinship among the goats. During my loneliest times, I wandered out to the barn to tell Kimikoi or Miah my tales of woe. They graciously shared their beds of straw and never seemed to mind when I used their soft bellies for pillows. The kids loved human contact. They chewed on my braids, sucked on my shirttail, and nibbled my nose and ears until I was driven to distraction with all the attention. The goats never let me down; they gave me constant companionship, in addition to all the dairy and meat products Bill and I needed to live.

Despite what I had heard people say about "stinky" goats, I found goat's milk and meat rich and fine-tasting. The goats gave more milk than we could possibly use, so I fed the excess to the dog, the cats, the chickens, and the hog. Even the vagrant skunk that bummed a room underneath the cabin turned sloppy fat from stealing milk from the dog's dish. Goat's milk meant more than just milk. We had whipped cream and butter, homemade ice cream and cottage cheese. Even the whey by-product, full of protein and acidity, was put to good use: it made a wonderful hair rinse.

When properly handled, goat's meat tasted as good as beef or wild game. After butchering, we hung the meat to age, and if the weather was cold enough, we ate it fresh. Otherwise we pressure-canned the choicest cuts, then sliced the tougher pieces to jerk-dry to take on camping trips. Goat heart and liver were good, but the small loin steaks, when floured and fried with eggs and potatoes for breakfast, were my favorite. The fat from the goats was edible, though it was not as palatable as hog lard or bear grease. It worked well, however, for making soap or as a softener and waterproofing agent for leather.

Though their intelligence made the goats agreeable and easy to train, it also got them into trouble. Fence-smart animals, they went over, under, or through any kind of barrier if there was something they wanted on the other side. We were fortunate enough to live miles away from other people's dogs, gardens, and short tempers, so I didn't worry about fencing the goats in. What we did do was fence off the garden and flower plots, so that they couldn't gain access to all the edible delicacies. The goats wandered freely, but they never ventured farther than the meadow or the woods surrounding the cabin and barn. They were not dummies. They knew that bears, coyotes, and lions prowled beyond the protection of the hound and Bill's rifle.

Natural climbers, the goats bounded up and down anything with height. Trucks, tractors, stacks of wood, mounds of dirt, bales of hay, benches, tables, or anything else that was climbable became fair game. I always got a kick out of seeing the whole herd on top of the twelve-cord woodpile. Each of them stood proud, as if they had just scaled Mt. Everest. They flew down en masse, turned, and raced back up to show off. All delightful fun, until the day three-month-old Korja got caught between two rounds of wood and snapped her leg in half. Bill shot her and skinned her. I tried to keep the other goats down

off the woodpile after that incident. They didn't listen. Climbing flowed in their blood, and they seemed to accept a casualty
or the prospect of injury as an acceptable part of the game.

The goats had more than their fair share of curiosity. This
mischievous trait made them poke their heads into absolutely
anything, and if that anything happened to be an open door or
window, they walked in and made themselves at home. One
morning I left two pumpkin pies cooling on the kitchen counter when I rode for the mail. I returned a half-hour later to find
the cabin door flung wide, two empty pie tins on the kitchen
floor, and Kimikoi curled up on the couch in front of the stove.
The only thing that topped that escapade was the night I raced
outside to help put out a runaway brush pile fire and returned
to find five culprits with front hooves on the table, their noses
in the still-hot-from-the-oven strawberry-rhubarb cobbler.

I had heard stories about mean and malicious goats, but we
never owned one. That's not to say there was not a very strict
pecking order within the herd. There were always certain does
who commandeered the kingpin positions and who bossed
everyone else. Even with seventeen head, we never had a goat
get injured by another goat. The Nubian buck, Mayo, was
mostly mild-tempered and friendly. He turned obnoxious and
bothersome during breeding season, but we could handle him
with strong words and a firm hold on his long ear. Though the
goats butted on occasion, they never gave us any reason to sus-
pect that the action meant anything more than "Pay attention
to me" or "Get out of the way."

Fairly easy keepers, the goats were not prone to disease or illness. We lost one doe and several kids at birthing, one doe to
old age, and the one doeling to a broken leg. We treated the
rare cough or minor infection with penicillin and loving care.
Given proper quantities of good hay and grain, plenty of salt
and fresh water, and a dry, draft-free place to sleep, the goats
thrived in good health.

The hardships were that they had to be fed and milked both morning and night, and if there were kids, they required feedings two to four times a day depending on their age. Kidding time could be fun if all went well, but when a doe decided to have her kids at the wrong time, it was another story.

When Miah decided to kid the first year I lived on the Northfork, she chose a clear, sunny March day when it was thirty-six degrees below zero. Bill was gone. When I went out to milk in the morning, Miah was in labor. When I returned to check on her a half-hour later, she was shivering so hard I brought out blankets to cover her. Two hours later, Miah still was trying to give birth, and I was half-frozen from running back and forth between the barn and the cabin. A novice midwife, I figured out that something was wrong. I leafed through my goat book, did some frantic reading, and tried my hand at delivery.

Exhausted from the labor, Miah barely moved as I reached inside her birth canal to find the problem. Soon I had hold of two tiny feet. With a little rearranging, a gentle pull on my part, and a huge push from Miah, the breech-birth buck was born. Because of the intense cold, I wrapped the reddish-brown fellow in a towel and rushed him back to the cabin for a quick cleanup, then made him a makeshift bed under the sink.

I worked with Miah all afternoon. Her labored breathing put fringes of crystalline frost on her eyelashes. The blood and mucus froze to her rump hair. Finally, at dusk, I delivered another buck and a tiny white doeling. By dark, I had managed to get the other chores done, and I half-walked, half-dragged poor Miah to the canning shed off the kitchen. I fixed her a bed and lit the old wood stove in hopes of reviving her body temperature and saving her life. Sadly, the little red buck had died. With frustrated patience, I coaxed milk into the other two kids. I ate a cold supper and crawled into bed, only to be awakened soon after by goat cries from the barn. I tromped outside in my nightgown and boots to find Kimikoi in a corner with three muddy newborns. Her kids had arrived a week early. The temperature claimed forty-five degrees below zero under a clear, velvety sky and a bright moon. I had no choice but to gather up the babies and pack them back to the cabin, clean them up, dry them off, and snuggle them in with Miah's two kids. Then I went back out to the barn to clean up Kimi, give her grain and warm water, and fix her a bed in a vacant stall. Dawn found me still working as I tried to convince the five kids to suck enough milk from a bottle to get started in life.

Miah survived that tortuous birthing, but she never regained her full strength. I milked her through the summer and raised her kids, but by autumn she was failing. I found her one evening folded under a pine tree, her bag shriveled and dry, too old and too tired to even open her eyes when I touched her face. I did not have the heart to butcher her or even dry her meat for the dog and cats. Bill gave me permission to take her to the edge of the woods for the coyotes and the bears.

Each goat, in his or her own way, taught me how to live my own life. They insisted on patience and understanding. They made me tougher and stronger in the face of loneliness and despair. They provided me with daily attention and gave me unconditional love. One by one, they presented me with a wealth of insight into animal nature. Plus they never asked for anything more than water, grass, to be milked, and a scratch behind the ears. The goats helped me believe in my budding creativity and paved the way for my writing career. Perhaps I loved them the most because they listened to me read my poetry, and they even appreciated my singing.

The first picture Laurie sent to Bill. Photograph by Gary Rowe.

William F. Atkinson, "Makwi Witco," at Val Halla, on the bank of the Northfork of the Flathead River in Montana, around 1977.

Laurie Wagner, "Little Fawn," at Val Halla, around 1977.

The Polebridge Store in the early 1970s.

Bill takes an early fall ride on War Eagle through Val Halla's lush
meadow in September 1976. The trees in the background are across
the river in Glacier National Park.

The workshop at Val Halla. The bags in front contain coal, which Bill used to forge knives. The light-colored pile in front is deer, elk, and moose hair that had been taken off the animal hides in preparation for braintanning. The goats loved to play on the woodpile.

Bill at the woodshed with a hundred-pound sack of beans or grain
across his shoulder. In his right hand he holds a beaver carcass. A
beaver plew laced into a willow hoop hangs on the slab wall.

Bill fleshing a beaver hide that has been laced into a round willow frame. He is wearing a handmade beaver and ermine hat. The Northfork of the Flathead River flows behind him. On the other bank is Glacier National Park.

Bill on Jere (Jeremiah). He is wearing a bearskin vest and a cross-fox and ermine hat.

Bill and Jere hauling hundred-pound sacks of beans and grain. Laurie
is wearing one of Bill's handcrafted knives. In the background,
snowshoes hang from a set of moose antlers.

Laurie wearing the ivory thunderbird Bill carved for her.

Laurie with Bill's mother, Catherine Atkinson, in the Bitterroot Mountains in 1981.

Laurie with twin Nubian goat kids in the Bitterroot Mountains.

Laurie and Bill in the Bitterroot Mountains.

Bill with Snook Moore at the Moore Ranch, Cora, Wyoming, in the winter of 1981–82.

Laurie with Mariko and her kids Kimikoi and Chitamico at the Flying A Ranch, Little Twin Creek, Cora, Wyoming, in April 1983.

Make a Joyful Noise

I come from a family of notoriously poor singers. That's not something one would usually brag about, but in our case it was something truly to be thankful for, because it brought us together in a good way. There wasn't a musical ear in our household during my growing-up years. Still, my family loved to sing in church on Sunday mornings, or on road trips when the miles got long and tempers turned cranky. We sang songs like "What a Friend We Have in Jesus" and "Swing Low, Sweet Chariot," or "Mairzy Doats" and "Over the River and Through the Woods." Singing was something we did whether alone in the shower or to the radio or together in a group.

I never knew how badly I sang until I joined the church choir and was exposed to lovely, melodious voices. I found out, much to my dismay, that I couldn't carry a tune in a bucket. I was stuck in that never-never land somewhere between a high alto and a low soprano. However, my inability to hit the right notes never diminished my love of song. Tolerant teachers and choirmasters appreciated my enthusiasm, if not my negligible talent. They simply placed me next to a friend with an exceptionally strong, true voice so that person could sing right into my ear to keep me on key.

For the Wagner family, Christmas was a favorite time to make a joyful noise. Dad was famous for dragging us door to door around Air Force base quarters on Christmas Eve to sing a rollicking, if tuneless, rendition of "We Wish You a Merry Christmas" to our neighbors. Gathered by the tree in the evenings, we played a game in which one person would call out a word such as "night" and someone else had to respond by singing an appropriate carol like "Silent Night" or "O Holy Night." Our repertoire of carols was endless, and all of us knew at least the first verse of every one. We always had a brightly decorated live Christmas tree even when we lived in tropical climes like the Philippines and Hawaii. Dad loved putting up festive lights and wrapping packages. He and Mom always invited an assortment of lone GIs and friends to our house to celebrate Christmas Day with an abundance of food, drink, and gifts.

When I burst out in song one Montana morning while dancing with the big white tomcat, Kriega, Bill put his hands over his ears and grimaced. "Please," he said, "don't sing." Even though he explained that hearing off-key notes was painful for a person with perfect pitch, he hurt my feelings. Bill had inherited that fabulous musical gift and had been trained in classical piano, while his brothers Bob and Dick played cello and violin. Their mother, Catherine, often had the young trio play for her lady friends at tea.

One of the first things Bill had brought to the cabin on the Northfork was an ancient upright piano. The log walls often shook with his virtuoso offerings of "Malagueña" or "Moonlight Sonata." He had been the leader of his unit's blue jacket choir at a naval air station in Washington State before he was sent to serve as a medic in Vietnam. In a fine tenor voice, he sang anything and everything: "Ebb Tide," "Unchained Melody," Faron Young's "Lillies Grow High," Marty Robbins's "The Blizzard." I loved hearing him sing and longed to join in, but he could not tolerate my voice. The minute I opened my mouth to sing, Bill's stony warning glare shut me down.

So I learned to sing alone while baking bread when Bill was off snowshoeing to check trap lines, or while milking the goats or weeding the garden. Since our closest neighbor, Old Tom, lived four miles away, I figured I wouldn't bother anyone when I sang at the top of my lungs while riding Jubilee. I also made the assumption that if my singing was that bad, perhaps it would keep the coyotes and bears from coming too close when I was off on one of my treks to pick up mail or get water from the spring.

When my first Christmas away from home rolled around, I felt bereft. No family. No celebration. No singing carols around the brightly lit tree. Bill brooked no joy on holidays. He assumed a solemn, nearly silent mien and kept to himself. Since we were snowed in and had no way to get into town to purchase gifts, plus no money, I made beaded ornaments from pinecones, grouse feather fans, pack rat tails, and beaver paws to mail to my parents and sisters. I made cards from construction paper and cut snowflakes out of typing paper. When Bill and I went to get a load of firewood, I sawed down a waist-high pine and threw it on top of the load. Back at the cabin, Bill promptly threw the tree to the ground, where the goats devoured it. He didn't have to tell me I was not allowed to decorate a holiday tree.

Christmas Eve arrived quietly. I had received numerous cards, greetings, and gifts from family and friends in the bi-weekly mail. The carols on the battery-powered radio brightened the day as I baked pies for the special meal the following day. I did my usual water hauling and wood chopping, and rationed out hay and grain for the horses and goats. The dog and cats received an extra helping of dry food soaked in warm goat's milk. I tried to share part of my faux joy with Bill, but he remained incommunicado at his desk, polishing antler rosettes to engrave.

As evening lengthened, my loneliness increased. I bundled up in my heavy coat and pack boots and put on gloves and a wool scarf to walk out and give the goats a goodnight treat. Black with below-zero cold, the night shimmered with the unreal brilliance of thousands of diamond-cut stars. A soft wind soughed in the tops of the lodgepoles that lined the path. Below the riverbank, icy water rushed over rocks.

The barnyard held the hush of a long-ago story. The trio of horses stood in a semicircle by an outdoor manger, steamy breath making halos of frosty air around shaggy heads. I peeked in the half-open barn door. Enough starlight seeped in for me to make out the does and the nearly grown kids curled together in sleep. Miah, the oldest doe, spotted me and raised her horned head. "Baaaa?" she asked, her thin blond beard wagging. "Muuh," I answered, and entered the sanctuary.

Each animal received an alfalfa cube and a gentle scratch behind the ears with a whispered "Merry Christmas." That's all it took for them to maul me with affection and shove snoopy noses in my pockets, their tiny hooves poking my thighs as they stretched up for more pats. A pile of loose hay in a middle stall provided a place for me to make a hollowed-out bed. The goats trooped in, too. The kids crawled into my lap and over my outstretched legs, nibbled at my hair, pulled at the pocket flaps on my coat, and sucked on my gloved fingers. Then they settled down like tired children, nestled where I could reach out and pet them. The does stayed standing and resumed chewing their cuds with half-closed eyes.

I softly sang "O Little Town of Bethlehem." The does cocked their ears. The kids bleated a tinny accompaniment. The curious horses stood to listen with their heads hanging over the half-door. I sang every Christmas carol I remembered from childhood. I stayed with my animal family until my intolerance for the cold drove me back to my human abode. I had a hard time saying goodnight to such an interested and respectful audience, and I had no doubt that they embraced the real message of the Christmas story better than any person. A burst of happiness filled my consciousness and replaced the haunting loneliness I had suffered all day.

I walked back to the darkened cabin with kid slobbers drying on my face. Upstairs, Bill had chosen to sleep solo and face his night horrors alone. An agnostic mother and a Protestant father had raised him in a divided family. He had been forced to participate in an unjustified and unholy war by an uncaring government. Like so many other young men, he had sacrificed part of his soul to survive. Though he remained a total mystery to my unschooled heart, I had begun to more fully comprehend why he sought a hard but simple life on the land. I understood better why he eschewed his fellow man and found peace with the animals, both wild and domestic. The four-footed ones had no religious platforms, no political postures, and no hidden agendas. They lived by instinct, and when their time came, they died without complaint.

Little by little, the black memories that haunted Bill began to shadow my sunny disposition. I found it harder and harder to maintain a semblance of childlike joy, and like a child I shied more and more from any action that might trigger his explosive anger or send him into a week-long depression. Eventually I quit singing, even to myself or the goats and horses. Silence became a safe refuge. For many years, my off-key but innocent voice stayed still. Vocal cords knotted with embarrassed fear, my throat ached even when I tried to speak.

Horseplay, Injuries, and Insults

I collected horse statues, read horse books, and played horses with other grade-school girls who were as horse-crazy as I was. As the middle of three daughters of an always-moving career Air Force father, my exposure to real horses was limited to occasional rides at nearby stables. The dull, sad circling of horses in dusty corrals and the keep-to-the-pathway plodding of dude rides disappointed my child's heart. My Christmas wish list read like this: a horse, a piano, and a room of my own. Poor Santa never had a chance at making me happy. But those three things came into my life when I arrived in the West.

I admit that I longed for the chance to freely straddle a horse almost as much as I did for Bill's embrace. He taught me how to ride by tossing me up bareback on Jere my first night in the mountains. The intense heat of the stocky paint's hide and the coiled energy of his muscles beneath my thighs made me take a death grip on his mane with both hands. "Relax," Bill said as he led the snorting gelding around the pole corral. "Horses smell fear. Jere's a bit much to handle, but he won't hurt you on purpose."

Bill insisted that I learn to ride without a saddle because he believed the skin-to-skin contact communicated the truest sensibility between human and horse. I watched in awe as Bill, clutching a rifle in one hand, grabbed reins and a hunk of mane in the other hand and vaulted onto the back of one of the horses. He relished an all-out gallop, and it was not uncommon to see him dashing around the meadow just for the sheer joy of riding. The horses loved him and came at his call, even from a mile or more away, to nose his pockets for carrots. They calmly succumbed three times each summer to shoeing, despite liberal amounts of Bill's sweat and a tangible blue streak of cuss words coloring the sky.

Bill had warned me early on that if I wanted to stay at Val Halla, it was mandatory for me to become an accomplished horsewoman. He insisted that I build my upper body strength in order to accomplish two important tasks: carry the five-gallon water bucket up the steep slope from the river and vault onto a horse bareback. I accomplished the first chore within a month. The second took me more than a year of daily practice, with sweet-tempered Ahkee standing sleepily as I repeatedly threw myself at his body, crashed into his side, and crumpled to the ground. Finally the day came when I managed to hook a heel over his back and claw my way astride. The whooping scream I let out made it sound as if I'd won an Olympic event and brought the other horses and goats running. Bill appeared at the cabin door polishing a piece of antler. He squinted and studied me sitting bareback on Ahkee, bouncing with childish delight. "Finally," he said, and walked back inside.

I grew fond of horsehair stuck to my thighs, the rich-wet stickiness of sweat and dirt on my rump, and the musky scent of horseflesh. I exhilarated in figure-eight canters over mown meadows and short forays through the trees to retrieve the mail. I cherished the trust that developed between the horses and me, all of whom I rode with only a hackamore.

Being the oldest and most experienced horse, Jubilee was seasoned enough to take my inexperience for granted. She taught me the tricks of the trade. Because I had no innate sense of direction, I often found myself lost within a mile of home. Going around in circles in thick timber or heavy willow bottoms, Jubilee would follow my inept reining as I searched for my back trail. She would wait until I gave up trying to figure out which way the cabin lay, then she would sigh like a drama queen, take control of the situation, and get us back to the barn.

One late spring day, Bill returned from an extended pack trip and said, "If you want company, Mark and Jammy will come visit, but they need fuel for their van. Take a gallon of gas up to them on Trail Creek. I stayed over with them last night."

I must have looked like I hadn't comprehend a word he said, because he led me to the tool shed, got a gas can off the shelf, filled it from a fifty-five-gallon barrel, screwed the lid on tight, and said, "Take the main road to the mailboxes. Turn right up Trail Creek. Go two or three miles. You can see their cabin from the road. Take Jubilee. She'll get you home again."

Jubes and I did fine for the first couple of miles; then she developed a serious limp in her right front foot. She acted as if putting her hoof down caused her incredible pain. Sitting bareback and either holding or balancing the gallon jerry can, I urged her forward with short jabs in the ribs. I didn't dare get off her back because I'd never be able to get back on again without the aid of a stump or a rock. As I mulled over my predicament, making slow time toward Trail Creek, a man stepped out of the timber and said, "What are you doing here?" Jubilee snorted and he backed up. I hadn't seen another person for some time, so his appearance out of nowhere unnerved me.

Faking boldness, I said, "I live here. What are you doing here?"

"Scaling timber. I work for the Forest Service. Lady, you scared the bejesus out of me. I had no idea anyone lived up here."

"Sorry," I said, slamming my heels into Jubilee's sides. As she rocketed ahead, I called back over my shoulder, "Gotta go." I had no desire to confess my adrenalin-boosted heart rate or chat with a stranger.

I made Mark and Jammy's with barely enough time to drop off the gas, drink some water, make a pit stop in the trees, and check Jubilee's foot. I could find nothing wrong. The sun had disappeared, and I had at least six miles to go to get home before dark. I promised Mark and Jammy a "spring's here" celebratory meal, and they agreed to come the next day. Miraculously, Jubilee's limp disappeared as soon as I headed her toward home. It took all my strength to rein in her renewed enthusiasm for galloping. I could not slow her down to a walk, and miles of her rocky trot rubbed my legs and backside raw. Bill did not inquire why I didn't sit down for supper. He handed me a foul-smelling concoction and said, "Now you know where the expression hard-ass comes from."

Messing around outside the cabin one fall evening, I swung myself up on Jere. Despite his wary glass eye and trail-hardened heart, he was gentle enough to indulge me. I had no intention of riding; it was too much trouble to walk out to the barn for a halter or bridle. I sat there enjoying the wind in the pine trees as the trio of horses picked at clumps of grass grown up through the pine duff. Suddenly, the woodshed door slammed behind Bill as he came outdoors. The horses spooked, racing off through the trees on a narrow, branch-burdened path. I should have slipped off Jere at his first lunge; instead I grabbed a double handful of mane and hung on. As Jere burst from the woods onto the meadow, the mare and stud colt thundering behind spurred him into an all-out, ears-laid-back gallop. In the excitement of the chase, I whooped and laughed until I saw, fast approaching, the three-foot-wide, five-foot-deep trench that marked the border crossing into Canada. Fun over, a wave of panic rushed down my spine at the steeplechase-type wreck ahead. The only thing my novice-rider brain could think to do was slide forward on Jere's outstretched neck and cup my hand over his eye. This gave him pause. He broke stride, then slowed enough for me to grip hand to wrist around his neck and drop. My feet bounced along the ground, Jere's front legs striking my legs until he stopped. Snorting, blowing hard, he rolled his wild eyes. On jellied legs and with shaking hands, I stripped off my shirt to tie around his sweaty neck and lead him back home.

Bill waited at the edge of the timber looking uncharacteristically pale. "I survived," I said, patting Jere's shoulder.

"It's a wonder you didn't break your neck. Don't do that again."

"I didn't do it on purpose," I retorted.

"Really?" he asked as if I'd staged the whole show to get attention.

I had learned early on that smarting off was like throwing gas on glowing embers. I kept my snotty response to myself. I had learned that listening, saying little, never complaining, and never thinking for a moment that going to the doctor was an option was the key to survival in Bill's world. And there were plenty of insults and injuries to endure.

Fingers whacked by an unwieldy ax as Bill tried to teach me to chop wood were my first injuries. Next, Ahkee spilled me in a deep snowdrift during a routine run for the mail, then stepped squarely on my instep. My foot swelled up to the size and color of an eggplant. Unable to wear either a sock or a boot, I swaddled the throbbing appendage in rags and wrapped it in a plastic bread sack to hobble out to do chores.

The time Jubilee's colt Sunshadow kicked me sticks in my craw like a fish bone. I had raised him, and he followed me like a dog. As I threw hay to the small horse herd, the weanling whirled and caught me above the knee with a hind hoof. I crawled to the cabin and wailed at the door until Bill appeared to scold, "You sound like a cat in heat. What's wrong now?" I explained my predicament through choking sobs. "Can you put weight on your leg?" he asked. I tentatively eased my balance over onto the injured limb. "Good. It's not broken," he said. "I told you to be careful around that colt. Treating him like a pet isn't smart. When's breakfast?"

When I sliced through the top of my thumb while trimming hooves, Bill poured peroxide on the bloody stump and folded the flap of skin back over the wound. "Hell, it's a long way from your heart," he said. Fishing around in a cupboard, he brought out a small metal box and extracted catgut, a curved suturing needle, a small syringe, and a bottle of Xylacaine. He said, "Close your eyes" and injected the numbing agent. Then he stitched me back together like a tattered quilt. "When did you have your last tetanus shot?" he asked. Knowing what was coming, I stuck out my tongue at him. With a sadistic smirk on his face, he took out another bottle, filled another syringe, and jabbed me in the shoulder. He made me a buckskin thumb protector lined with marten fur, and I learned how to milk and do dishes one-handed.

Romantic interludes balanced out the daily routine and minor mishaps. Sometimes we rode to gather sage from a flat downriver, or to pick mint from the beaver slough or huckleberries from the slopes. Once at sunset we meandered our way to a giant curve in the river where a deep hole had been carved out by the current. We swam the horses through the deep water and emerged soaking but laughing. Then we turned around and swam them back across just for the thrill of feeling their huge bodies float and their powerful legs work the water. Only once did Bill take me on an overnight pack trip. Settled in our blankets under a canvas tarp with the horses tied close by to alert us in case a grizzly happened past, I asked Bill why he didn't take me with him more often when he went into the backcountry. "Because you are too much of a distraction," he said and kissed me.

I spent hours currying the horses and days cleaning the barn and corrals, but Bill's horses would never be mine. Although I shared his equine dreams, I did not possess my own. Jubilee slunk a foal; Ahkee was injured and shot, and he would not be the last. Bill bought Eagle to breed Jubilee, and the brute took a hunk out of my thigh when I was riding Jere one day. I had never given up on my girlish dream to have my own horse, but dreams had a way of being hard to hold.

Bear Information

More than a century before I moved to the Northfork, a grizzly mauled a mountain man named Hugh Glass. The story of his crawl back to civilization became a legend. A little more than a decade before, a grizzly had killed two young women in Glacier National Park. The account of their deaths in *Night of the Grizzly* became a nationwide best seller. In 1976, a year after my arrival, another girl was dragged from her tent in a park campground and killed. Needless to say, my parents expressed their dismay about my chosen territory when they wrote to me.

Less than a year later, the infamous Giefer Grizzly was trapped on the Southfork of the Flathead, where he was a known cabin molester. Game and Fish officials turned him loose on the Northfork, where he continued his escapades. The Giefer wasn't a killer. He merely smashed windows, tore doors off hinges, and helped himself to the Crisco, the catsup, and other supermarket delicacies. Not only did he make local headlines for months, but *Sports Illustrated* also published his story.

One spring, while standing on the bank of the Northfork where the river tumbled in broken rapids across the U.S.-Canadian border, I thought of Hugh Glass's crawl, the Giefer Grizzly, and the girls who had died. I thought about the grizzly stories I had heard, and about each of the seven grizzlies I had seen in the wild. But mostly I thought about the she-bear not far from me.

She lay motionless, her golden fur blending with the autumn ground cover of tamarack needles and cottonwood leaves. Silver-tipped guard hairs spread over her massive hump and down her back like morning frost. Her half-open eyes were glazed, and her wide nostrils fluttered with a bare gesture of life. One giant forepaw stretched wide, the curved five-inch claws digging into the earth. Curled tight to her chest, the other forepaw had been chewed raw by a steel snare.

Behind her, in a patch of leafless brush, a cub moaned and cried. Before her, more than a dozen thousand-dollar cameras clicked away, while whispered voices inquired about the lasting quality of the tranquilizer. The she-bear lay motionless while they measured her length, judged her weight, pulled a sample tooth, tagged her ear, and finally collared her with a radio transmitter. In a few hours, when the drug wore off, she was supposed to rise and resume her natural life.

I wondered if she would ever walk again. And if she did, would she be able to successfully forage with a damaged paw and a missing tooth? And if she could, how long would it be before the beep of the transmitter betrayed her to another scientific experiment? I didn't stay to find out. As I waded across the river, I glanced back once at her golden body surrounded by men and four-wheel drives. I wished her dead rather than see her again at the mercy of man.

Not long after, I saw a photograph of a painting that depicted a forest scene where a huge grizzly lay with two arrows in its chest. A young Indian in a breechcloth leaned over the

bear with one hand on its massive head. The Indian blew
smoke from a pipe into the bruin's nostrils to make a sacred
offering for the bear's spirit. I sensed a miraculous understanding of instinctual communication, and a profound spiritual
connection between the Indian and the bear.

I lived with the image of the golden she-bear being treated as
a piece of research data and with the news of park bears that
killed and were killed in turn. The Giefer was finally shot down
as he rooted in a garbage dump.

It was a hard knowledge, the kind that haunted the corridors
of my mind and prowled around the corners of my heart. It
was the knowledge of alienation, the realization that men and
women were no longer vital, functioning entities in the natural
world. The bulk of us lived in houses separated from the earth
by concrete and walls, insulation and air-conditioning. The few
who did touch the earth took campers and tents, down-filled
sleeping bags and freeze-dried food. They ventured out for a
few days or a few weeks, and they looked, listened, walked, and
then returned to close themselves off again from the earth that
sustained them.

Often I lay on the ground trying to feel the heartbeat that
I knew was hidden within the earth. The Indian lay thus for
centuries. But now other sounds, other vibrations, mask that
beating: the myriad roars of vehicle, computer, and tickertape.
What the Indian and the grizzly once shared no longer existed.
What was once worshipped was now used irreverently, with little spiritual thought or conscience. I felt so far away, that I had
been gone for so long, that the earth and I spoke two separate
languages. The alienation ran deep. My roots hung dried and
frayed.

∽

When I shared these observations about the she-bear by writing an article for the Student Action Committee newspaper at

the University of Montana, the following letter to the editor appeared the next week:

∽

We Americans champion good old Yankee ingenuity but seldom understand or advocate research. Government investment in research is falling rapidly, especially under the present administration. Wildlife research is at its lowest ebb in decades.

The problem, at least partially, is based on the misconception that biologists are people who torment wildlife. The recent article in The SAC *by Laurie Wagner helped perpetuate this warped image of biologists. Her account of a bear research project in British Columbia distorts the scene, the event, and the intent, all in one page of biased evaluation. . . .*

Although Ms. Wagner's article conveys a conservation ethic, which is good, it is also another example of exploitive journalism. It is unfortunate that people must use and abuse the grizzly bear for the emotionalism it stirs. Last year's maulings in Glacier National Park made national headlines, yet how many people heard about the fourteen-year-old boy who was "ripped apart" by dogs near Champaign, Illinois, last December? Or the murder every thirty minutes in the USA?

Please, let's keep journalism, and wildlife, in a more realistic perspective.

∽

Charles Jonkel and seven of his research assistants signed the letter.

I had no idea that my naïve but heartfelt thoughts about bears would cause an uproar. The next week I sent a letter of explanation in response to the paper:

༄

*It seems Dr. Jonkel has misread both the content and the
purpose of my essay . . . [which] was not written or sub-
mitted for publication as a piece of "journalism." I am not
a reporter and I made no attempt . . . to cover the news by
stating names or dates as factual. . . . My essay is charged
with emotionalism because what I feel for the grizzly is emotional, not scientific.*

*I did not intend to give a "warped image" of biologists or
wildlife research. . . . I had hoped that my essay would make
people stop and question their present personal relationship
with the earth. I regret that Dr. Jonkel missed the point.*

༄

Because we lived in grizzly country, Bill taught me how to be
aware of everything going on around me whenever I stepped
out the door. I never walked or rode first through the woods—
he did, and I followed. He pointed out bear scat on the trails
and bear markings on the trees. He told me stories of his
own encounters with both black bears and grizzlies. We once
watched a young black bear rustling through the old dump at a
homestead. He found a rusted, dented lard can and managed
to pry the lid off, and though the ancient contents must have
been rancid, he entertained us by lying on his back and holding the can in his paws, trying to wedge his head in far enough
for his tongue to reach the fetid dregs. One fall, Tom from the
Homeplace Ranch downriver came nine miles to tell us that a
goat we had given him had been pulled out the barn window
by a grizzly, killed, and hauled off. He had followed the drag
sign until he found the half-eaten carcass buried under duff
and leaves and the bear's tracks disappearing into the river. Old
Tom was so deaf that he hung pots and pans from his doors
and windows so he would be sure to hear a bear breaking into
his cabin. He drove over one day on his rickety three-wheeler

to report that a rogue bear had been there in the night, demolished part of his empty meat shed, and smashed in his kitchen door before Old Tom felt rather than heard the commotion and turned on his flashlight to see the hulking shape in the dim glow. His startled shout sent the bear hightailing back out the way he had come in.

Bill found the bottom half of the door at the lodge upriver bashed in, claw marks on all the logs under the windows, the door of the propane refrigerator wrenched open, dishes smashed and scattered, and the back door blasted off. The only real damage was a mutilated empty catsup bottle. By and large, the hound alerted us to too-close bears, and the bears, wary of dogs and humans, stayed away.

Bill showed me how to skin the bear he shot, how to hold the thick hair and hide away from the flesh and slice precisely so that I would leave the fine leaf lard on the body and not score the pelt that he would later stretch and tan. The naked body of the beast hanging from the beam in the open-ended log garage looked like a man with a bad sunburn. Bill used the brains for tanning, boiled out the skull, and removed the teeth to make a necklace. He kept the claws as well. The heavy but soft robe kept me warm during the coldest winter nights. Bear ham and bear sausage filled our breakfast plates along with fresh eggs and sourdough biscuits.

Every morning for months, I watched Bill go through the motions of setting a gigantic bear trap that was traditionally set by using C-clamps. The instrument, a mesmerizing hunk of black iron and chain, fascinated me. Trapping bears had been outlawed, and owning a bear trap was illegal. The dang thing was so heavy that I couldn't lift it or drag it, so I swept and mopped around the odd contraption. With one foot on each wide spring, Bill would lean over, grasp the closed jaws one in each hand, clench his teeth, bow his back, and wrench the trap open. The veins on his neck stood out, the muscles in his arms and shoulders bulged, and a great woof of air, not unlike the grunt of a bear, would escape from his lungs as he shifted his feet to hold down the jaws and set the trigger on the round pan. Then, satisfied that he was still in shape, he would step aside, grin, and go outside for a length of stove wood, which he dropped on the pan to spring the trap. The smashing clang of the snap rattled the windows and made my teeth ache. Urging me to practice, to learn how to set the trap myself, Bill often told me the following story:

Once a white man lived with a squaw in the mountains. He was bad-mannered and ill-tempered, a loathsome brute who mistreated the woman when she did not do his bidding. She grew to hate his hands on her, grew to despise the way he beat her when he had had too much to drink. She did not cringe, or cry, or try to run away. Instead, when he was off running trap lines for coyote and beaver and lion, she worked and worked to learn how to set the big bear trap that he kept out in the wood-shed. It took her months to get confident enough and strong enough to be able to set the trap every time she tried. Then she waited. She waited for a winter night when it was forty below zero, when the stars winked her conspiracy in the cold heavens. After the man had gone to bed, and knowing his regular routine of getting up in the middle of the night to go to the outhouse, she carried the bear trap to the path behind the cabin, wired it to a large pine tree, and secured it with many twists and wraps. Then, hands burning on the icy iron, she set the trap where she was certain the man would step. Safe back inside, still dressed, she lay under her blankets and listened. She heard the man moan and rise. Heard him go down the stairs in the dark. Heard him open the door and go outside. She even heard his footsteps crunching on the snow. She waited, holding her breath, and when she heard the trap trip and his throat-gargled scream, she grabbed a pack of clothes and supplies she had pre-pared, strapped on a pair of snowshoes, and strolled away.

The story stayed with me. I wanted to be that woman, a woman who never got angry, just got even.

Sunshadow

The buckskin had been born in late spring just as the flies were beginning to get bad. As Bill was shoeing War Eagle, he had Jubilee tied close by to keep the restless stud calmed down. Jubes, usually quiet and steady, fussed and stomped and strained at her lead rope. Bill shushed her a few times and then noticed that she was trying to foal. He led her to the corral and turned her loose. Within the hour she was licking her slick colt clean, and the little buckskin was trying to get his long legs lined out so he could nurse. Bill gave me the colt, and I named him Eagle's Sunshadow. Between the two of us, Bill and I broke him to halter, taught him some manners, and tried to keep him from becoming a raucous idiot in the midst of the goats, dog, cats, and skunks that frequented the barn.

We never knew how he got injured, but Bill guessed that Mayo butted him full in the chest during a playful match of king-of-the-dunghill. A cyst blossomed under the skin at the point of Sunshadow's shoulder. Bill treated the growth with herbs and oils, but it grew to the size of a volleyball, inhibiting the buckskin's movement and causing him pain. With his medic's experience and drugs given to him by a veterinarian friend, Bill put the colt under, wrapped a cloth around his eyes, and began to excise the lump. I ran back and forth between the wood stove in the kitchen and the yard, carrying red-hot irons to sear the cut blood vessels.

After an hour of surgery, it became clear that the growth was a bone-deep abscess gone cancerous. It had infiltrated muscles and ligaments. If Bill removed the tumor, the colt would be permanently crippled. If he didn't remove it, Sunshadow would be crippled anyway, or would possibly die from infection. I begged Bill to take the colt to town for a second opinion, but he argued that the trip would be too traumatic for a horse that had never been taught to load or ride in the stock truck. Besides, even if we could afford the hundreds of dollars in bills, it was doubtful a vet could do anything either.

I slammed my way into the cabin and stood at the window crying as Bill led the still-drugged colt with halting steps into a copse of aspen. I heard two shots. Later Bill told me that he had placed the rifle against a straight-trunked tree, sighted it on the axis joint behind the dark ears, pulled the trigger, and missed. Shocked at his ineptitude (Bill never missed a shot), he walked up to the colt, who was looking at him with sleepy eyes, and shot him point-blank. He walked back home carrying the fresh-skinned buckskin hide and Sunshadow's long black tail.

❧

The stench of rotting horseflesh drew the bears. Bill went daily to check the carcass, hoping to get a shot and secure bear meat for the winter. None came. With studied patience, he hung what was left of the colt's haunch in an old outhouse and set twin bear traps on the floor. All night he waited. All day he waited. We were eating supper when the most god-awful roar erupted across the meadow. Bill grabbed his rifle and ran, shouting for me to stay back. I locked the dog in the cabin and followed, sprinting my way through the trees. I found Bill breathless, his back against an aspen as he fought to calm his lungs. Twin two-year-old cubs had fought to get to the meat. Both had been caught by a front leg in different traps. They were in the process of tearing apart the outhouse and each other. "Stay here," Bill ordered. "Right here. Can you reach that branch? Good. If anything goes wrong, you go up the tree. Agreed?" I nodded, stretching my arm up to see if I could grip the limb. I watched him walk forward, rifle at his hip. Then I heard two shots, one right after the other, and he hollered for me to come.

The bears lay atop each other, half-clutched in an embrace. The bullets had severed the tops of their spines, leaving only a small hole in each hide. After Bill released them from the traps, we pulled them out into the sunshine, where their summer-sheened hides glistened and rippled in the wind. One was a cinnamon, the other a blond. "Go get the truck," Bill said. "We'd better get them out of here before their ma comes looking for them." He left the rest of the horsemeat as an offering for other bears.

We worked all night and all the next day skinning and butchering the bears, then canning the meat. Bill fleshed and dried the hides, leaving the heads and claws on the robes. All winter, for hours a day, he worked the pelts, using great care with the difficult tanning process. He never verbalized his emotionally intent endeavor, but I understood his sadness over the colt, and knew his remorse over taking young twin bears when he had bargained for only one mature boar. I stood by when Bill cut the ropes that held the bearskins in their log frames. I helped him pull the nylon cord through the holes outlining each fur.

When the hides were free, Bill held up the blond pelt to me, and I grasped the bear in my arms, head on my shoulder, front paws dangling near my waist, back paws dragging the floor. I breathed in the bear's scent, the wild musk that overrode the sweet-sick scent of brains and sweat. I had eaten the bear's heart and liver. I had rendered the fat for making piecrusts and biscuits. I had served his tender meat with onions and garlic, savoring the rich gravy over mashed rutabagas and turnips. I danced the bear around the room, our spirits waltzing, and found the intense sacred connection between man and beast that I had longed for.

Executing a near-perfect curtsy, I smiled as Bill took my partner from me. He still had to stitch a canvas skirt to the hide and then slow-smoke the softened inner flesh over a cherry-wood fire. Marked by the experience that had created an indelible bond between the bear and me, I wished Charles Jonkel and his assistants the same rare opportunity. What would their research show if they too breathed in the last breath of a bear, ate the flesh, wore the warm robe, and cavorted with the bear's spirit? What blessings might occur if people could rediscover their close connection to the bears, to the earth where they roamed?

Bread, Beer, and Old Tom

Bread wasn't my strong suit. While I knew a lot about English literature, philosophy, religion, sociology, and the humanities, I knew very little about cooking or baking. "Neophyte," I think, was the word Bill used to describe my skill level in the kitchen as well as the outdoors. I preferred that to "inept." Despite his teasing assertions to the contrary, I honestly did know how to boil water. As a boy, Bill had taken over the kitchen to make French toast each Sunday morning for the family. His culinary expertise grew with the years he spent alone in the backwoods. Sourdough creations became his specialty.

I taught myself the basics by reading cookbooks and following recipes for cookies, cakes, muffins, biscuits, pancakes, and cornbread. With some special effort, I learned to roll out a fine bear-grease piecrust. But bread-making eluded me. I turned out shrunken loaves with soggy bottoms and rolls that could have doubled as hockey pucks. It became an ongoing challenge in the cabin, with Bill saying that the only way to make bread was to "simply do it."

One late winter morning as I hurried to gather the ingredients for a batch of bread, I grumbled over all the chores that I still had to do outdoors, in particular shoveling out the windows, which had been blocked by huge drifts of roof-tumbled snow. I thought my mumbling would prompt Bill to volunteer to do the shoveling and let in some much-needed light. Instead, he said he would make the bread so I could get outside and enjoy the fresh air.

Several hours later, with four long windows dug clean, I came back inside the cabin drenched in sweat and fingering the budding blisters on my hands. The kitchen was now lit with streamers of bright snow-reflected sunlight. Bill was leaned back in his chair eating a huge cinnamon roll studded with walnuts and raisins and dripping with goat's butter and honey. A perfect loaf of golden-brown bread cooled on the counter.

"Help yourself," Bill said, his expression blithe, devilish, and self-satisfied.

"How do you do it?"

"This time I used some sourdough, a dollop of bear grease, some salt and honey, a little yeast, and a little soda."

"I still don't see how you do it without a recipe or measuring cups."

"Old Tom taught me the basics years ago." Bill licked his fingers.

Old Tom Reynolds was a lifelong bachelor and a retired Forest Service cook. In his mid-seventies, he lived alone in a charming chalet-style cabin he had built himself on a quarter section of timbered land he had homesteaded years before. We didn't see Old Tom often, but sometimes we would ride horseback cross-country to visit him. One time our stop-to-chat coincided with his bread-baking day. He gave us four huge rolls to bring home. Old Tom never baked his bread in loaves. He said a loaf dried out long before he could eat it. Instead, he made rolls out of his bread dough, filling a nine-by-thirteen-inch pan with six to eight perfectly sculpted mini-loaves.

Even though I had heard through the grapevine that Old Tom disapproved of my living with Bill without the sanction of being married, I thought he might agree to be my ally in mastering the art of bread-making. I left a polite note in his mailbox on the dirt road that sat a mile down off the mountain from his cabin. With humility, I asked for his bread recipe. He replied by mail, stating that sharing recipes wasn't something he usually did, but in his neat, precise, British-style handwriting were two recipes. #1: One sifter white flour, one sifter wheat flour, one heaping cup dry milk, one-half to three-fourths cup lard, four eggs, three tablespoons wheat germ, three tablespoons sugar, two teaspoons salt, one tablespoon yeast, two dippers water. #2: Two packages yeast, two cups scalded milk, one-fourth cup butter, one-half cup sugar, two teaspoons salt, two eggs, six and a half cups white flour, one cup of raisins.

Not exactly sure how much a sifter or a dipper contained, I felt too shy and embarrassed to ask. I guesstimated and began to practice with religious fervor. Still I could not figure out the secret to making decent bread. Homemade bread was not a luxury for us; it was a staple. Bill normally went to town only twice a year, once in the spring and again in the fall to stock up before first snow by purchasing or trading for hundredweight sacks of flour, along with sugar, salt, and honey. It took me years to figure out that making good bread took four secret ingredients that would never be found in any written recipe: love, time, patience, and warmth. Bread dough was like having a baby to care for. I had to tend it constantly. It took time to mix and stir and knead. Time for the yeast to work and rise. Time to shape the rolls or loaves and let them rise again. Time for baking. Time for cooling. It took strong hands and plenty of arm muscle to work the dough. It took strong discipline not to eat a whole loaf of golden-crusted hot bread in one sitting. If Bill or Old Tom had told me those things in the beginning, I would not have had so many bread disasters.

❧

Old Tom softened toward me and rather grudgingly gave over
to the idea that I was a good gal, even if my morals were highly
questionable. He liked that I had a college education and was an
avid listener to his stories. He also loved the fact that I had been
born in Edinburgh, Scotland; he therefore considered us
kinsmen. Born in England, Tom Reynolds served in the Royal
British Army during World War I and jumped ship in India. He
headed for Canada, where he herded sheep, eventually working
his way down into the U.S. He made the Forest Service his
career by working seasonally, saved his money, bought his land,
built his cabin in an aspen clearing surrounded by deep pine
woods, and lived there in happy seclusion.

Locals called Old Tom "the grand old gentleman," and he
was. Whenever we visited, he offered us a cup of tea or a glass
of his homemade beer or wine, along with the homemade buns
or a piece of pie. He loved classical music, which he played on
his battery radio at maximum volume to compensate for his
increasing deafness. I learned that he had once played with the
London Philharmonic. Well educated and very well read, he
invariably had a *Smithsonian* or *National Geographic* open on
the table where he spent much of his time near the wood cook
stove in a sunny alcove off the kitchen. He hardly ever went to
town, maybe once a year, but he was a people person, a good
conversationalist, and he loved visitors at any time.

Old Tom never married and didn't care to have a dog or cat,
but he usually had a parakeet or two in residence with him in
his hideaway. Livestock wasn't his forte either. The chicken
house he began in his early days on the Northfork was never
finished. Old Tom said he figured the resident bear population
was enough for him to deal with without coaxing them in
closer with tasty domestic animal morsels. Most years, he
supplemented the store groceries delivered by the mailman
with moose meat.

We didn't see Old Tom often. He occasionally rode over on his three-wheeler, and he always had a bit of local gossip to share along with some magazines that he thought we'd enjoy. Even though Bill and I would eventually leave the Northfork, our close friendship with Old Tom survived. We hauled twelve cords of wood up to him and gave that to him along with Bill's ancient pickup as a good-bye gift. Throughout the years, no matter where I landed, I loved getting letters from Old Tom.

∾

Dear Laurie,
I hope you are doing well and keeping well and still working in cattle country. Nothing doing here this year, but in '88 there was a bad fire close to Polebridge. Several cabins went up in smoke but they saved the store. The big trees there were killed and even the pole bridge caught fire and fell in the river. In the spring last year millions of mushrooms sprang up and a lot of people from all over came to pick and sell them. A buyer was there and gave good money for them. One man said he made enough to put down $2,000 on a new car. The wolf project is still in progress with the wild-life biologist, Diane Boyd, in charge. She's living in the cabin you used to live in. A couple of wolves have given trouble south of the park; on one ranch they killed two calves and have not yet been caught. The rancher was remitted for the loss. I think someone will shoot them and keep their mouth shut.
My Kind Regards,
Tom

∾

Fourteen years after I had last seen him, I got a final letter from Old Tom. He wrote me at the age of ninety-five:

∾

Dear Laurie,

I'm sorry I'm so late answering your letter. I've got no excuses, just old age, laziness. This winter is the mildest I can remember, not too much snow and only two times when the temperatures went close to zero. We will have an early spring and I won't grumble about that. I think I wrote to you that my friend [the Canadian] Joe Bush died and we held last rites in June. One of his grandsons spread his ashes in a line and I watered them with a six-pack. I thought he would have liked the beer better than flowers. I don't know if you remember the story of Charlie Wise and Washburn. They were joking one night and drinking beer about who would die first; if Charlie died first, Washburn would bring a case of beer with him when his time came; if Washburn died first, Charlie would bring a case with him when he died. The next morning they were still joking about it when Washburn went out to feed the horses. He was a long time coming back in to breakfast, so Charlie went out to see what was holding him up and found Washburn dead on the hay-stack. You can imagine the shock that was to him, after joking about death. I don't know where Charlie is buried, but I'm sure he took no beer with him. . . . I'm about as usual. I can still climb my hill with groceries on my back, but it's getting tough.

Love,

Tom

❧

The Christmas card and letter I sent to Old Tom in 1993 came back ten days later marked "Deceased." The kind postmistress wrote on the back, "Tom passed away at home, December 14th." Another friend sent me his obituary from the Kalispell paper. Old Tom had only one surviving relative, a nephew in Australia. The paper said that he had died at home in his own bed, held by his close and special friend, the mail carrier, Becky Green. They flew the flag at the Polebridge Store at half-mast for a week in honor of Old Tom. A memorial service, similar to the one the community had had for his friend Joe Bush, was planned for the spring. I hoped that someone would think to take a six-pack of beer to water Old Tom's ashes. I prayed that the grand old gentleman had taken his recipe for home brew to the other world. If I could have attended the service, I would have taken a loaf of fresh homemade bread made from one of his recipes. With no little effort, I had become a great baker of breads, even to the point of grinding my own wheat and milling oats for different flours. I especially enjoyed making pans of cracked wheat honey mini-loaves to give as gifts to friends. If bread remained the staff of life, then surely friendship stood a close second.

First Run

Climbing into a canoe with Bill when he had a perfectly good reason to want to kill me seemed a foolish thing to do, but I did it anyway.

My third Northfork winter, finally conceding to spring, permitted the entrenched snow banks to retreat until the only remaining white was on the lee side of the cabin and barn, and on the north slopes of ridges. The river ran high, turned the color of weak coffee, and lapped the banks under newly leafed cottonwoods. Restless after months of being captive to house chores and the slow pace of snowshoes, I didn't hesitate when Bill asked, "Run the river with me?"

"Yes," I said. "When?"

"Tomorrow morning. Early. Dress warm."

"Okay," I nodded, watching his broad shoulders disappear into the living room.

The first words to pass between us in over a week echoed in the sunlit kitchen, where I was making grizzly cookies, a special recipe that included bear grease and dried huckleberries.

Spooning mounds of dough onto baking sheets, I wondered if I had been wise to agree to go. Bill and I were at terrible odds again, but the river called. Its siren voice, so long stifled by ice, was singing a new song. I wanted to know it, to feel more of the river than just the ferocious tug it delivered each time I slid down the muddy bank and walked the thick plank to dip buckets in the roiling current.

A river rat from Florida, Bill had canoed for years on everything from slow-moving bayous and mile-wide waterways to wild whitewater rivers like the Northfork that rushed a hundred feet outside our door. For years I had listened to stories of his running the river's course from the border to Polebridge. Intrigued, I had waited a long time for the same chance. Suburb-raised, with no water experience beyond a childhood paddleboat float on a pond, I swallowed a lump of apprehension and chased it with a wad of raw dough. Of whom was I more afraid, Bill or the river? Bill's unpredictable moods always left me in a tailspin. One day I was his friend, the next his enemy. One moment he worshipped my feminine allure, the next he turned on me with misogynist fury. No matter what I did to try to assuage his volatile temper, I never knew with whom I was going to wake up each morning. He could be seductive and charming or foul-mouthed and irritated. I did not know if he suffered from manic depression, post-traumatic stress disorder (words I would not learn until years later), or some other malady. I just knew I needed to watch my step and my tongue, constantly wary of what might pull the pin on an explosive outburst. The idea of going with him on the river sent shivers up my spine. The notion of not going made my heart ache. Now or never, a voice said in the far reaches of my mind. Now or never.

Clad for the cold, I stood by the river as Bill and his friend Jim carried the eighteen-foot cedar canoe from the shed to the water. Jim, who had known Bill since the Bob Marshall Wilderness days and had been staying in one of the guest cabins upriver, said, "Morning," and tipped his hat to me. He lowered the stern of the sleek craft into the chop as Bill pushed to float the boat into a pool. Holding the bowline taut against the current, Bill motioned for me to get in. Jim touched my shoulder as he walked past. He asked, "Okay?" Hesitant to speak or meet his sapphire eyes, I nodded my head yes. "Careful," he said. He called our half-shepherd, half-bloodhound Kyote to follow him and walked up the bank.

Bill pulled the canoe in closer, held the bow firm with one hand, and reached out with the other to steady me as I stepped one careful foot at a time into the middle, staying low. Balancing by gripping the sides, I crept to the bow and sat down just as he said, "Good girl." He tossed the line at my feet, shoved off, and slid into the stern. Those two words of unexpected praise flushed my cheeks as the Northfork grabbed the canoe and sucked us downstream.

"Here," Bill said, poking me in the hip with a paddle. I glanced over my shoulder, hurried to put on my gloves, and reached back as he said, "Hold it like this." I took note, then swiveled forward as the canoe ducked into the first small rapid. "Paddle right," he yelled over the gargle of the water. I shoved the paddle in on the right side. "Too deep; pull up on it, there you go. Nice and easy or you'll wear yourself out." His deep voice, muffled by the river's liquid slaps, sounded almost kind. Perhaps, somehow, he would find a way to forgive me for my latest transgression and things would be okay again.

Moving swiftly through a wide chute, we rounded a curve, and the cabin vanished. As the only surety and comfort I knew disappeared, I tried to swallow the cotton caught in my throat. Foreign and frightening, everything ahead excited and terrified me. Each nerve ending tingled. Sensations rippled past: a buttermilk sky giving way to periwinkle blue, trees whisking by, a vocal raven winging over, boulders breaking water into white spray looming until Bill steered around them. Finally, after days prickled with anger and nights curled cold in separate beds, I wanted to talk. I ached to shout back, "Please don't hate me. Pull over. Stop. I need to know what you're thinking." But it was too late. We were caught in the river's spiraling vortex, and there was no turning back. We couldn't return upstream if we wanted to. We were going down, and nothing would stop us now.

Bill called, "Stroke . . . stroke" in measured cadence, and I picked up the beat, paddling in time with his rhythm. Images of the past month flashed past in freeze-frame shots: Bill and Jim swapping stories of Vietnam or packing in the wilderness; tales of the best way to break a mule; recitations on how to forge a knife. Bill's cabin fever sarcasm. Jim offering to bring wood in for me. Bill alluding to a woman he saw in town. Jim helping me clean the barn. Bill criticizing my soggy bread or burned biscuits. Jim saying they were delicious. Bill arguing with me. Jim kissing me on the cheek while tears plopped into cold dishwater. I choked on the emotional logjam—the debris of fierce loving and senseless fighting piled up into a haphazard dam that had no other option but to bust loose and give way. I wanted to scream: "I slept with him because he wanted me. You had stopped talking to me or touching me. He's kind and you're cruel."

"Hard left," Bill hollered. I dug the paddle into the current on the left side, but the river evaporated out from under my thrust. "Faster! . . . Now!" My eyes shot up in time to see everything explode into a storm of silver sparkles. A wall of water whapped me. Certain that I was going to die, I shrieked. Bill whooped, a cry of sheer joy that echoed off the squat rock cliff that appeared ghostlike through falling mist. The canoe slewed sideways, heading for a full-length smash.

"Hard left!" I shoved once, twice, pushing all my weight into the effort. On the third shove I closed my eyes and mouthed "God save me." I felt the paddle clip the stone's pocked face just as Bill dug in and swung us in a leaping surge to the right. The canoe reared, then plunged into a trough. Another wave, this one thundercloud dark, curled above me, and somehow I had the presence of mind to force my left hand into a death grip on the paddle and reach out with my right for the gunwale.

Spotting daylight, able to breathe again, I found myself flat on my back in the bottom of the canoe, the paddle floating beside me in six inches of water. "Bail," Bill said, laughing, as he pulled a half-gallon lard can out of the rucksack. Drenched, shivering, relieved to be alive, and terrified, I couldn't see anything to be jolly about. Bill, however, danced in his seat, his paddle tucked between his knees as he pulled off his buckskin shirt, wrung it out, and stuffed it in the sack.

"Ee haw!" he hollered, waving the paddle above his head before he went back to work, digging in on both sides of the canoe as I kneeled facing him, dipping and dumping as fast as I could.

"Bill?" I began. The smile between his black beard and mustache stiffened. His eyes narrowed—a stern warning not to talk. I inched around so I wouldn't have to watch the muscles rippling in his bare shoulders; his nipples peaked from the cold. I bailed until I couldn't scoop anymore, then settled on the bow seat, my fingers purple-red and too stiff to handle the paddle. Hunched up, miserable, I tried to focus on the nine o'clock sun, which was working hard to thaw my now hatless and very wet head.

"Paddle," Bill said, that too-well-known tinge of an order in his voice. I swung around to glare at him. He added, "It will warm you up. And take off your jacket and sweater; the sun will dry you faster." I bit my lip to stifle the smart-ass retort that hung on my tongue and did as he said. Then, furious that he was right, I paddled faster and faster until I was panting with exertion.

"Keep it up," Bill said, "and you'll regret it. Miles and miles to go."

I forced myself to settle down, trying to concentrate on the scenery flashing by as the canoe crow-hopped through a series of tiny rapids. Each bend of the river revealed different land-scapes: sage flats, aspen groves, feeder creeks, a backwater where a bull moose stood drinking, here and there a cabin tucked back in the jack pine. My frantic dreams of the night before faded. The gossip I had heard that his first woman dis-appeared and was never heard from again quit replaying itself in my head. The notion that Bill would kill me, then cover up the murder by making it look like an accident, fled. Sure, the locals called him "Wild Bill" and "Crazy Bill," and he had a reputation for being psychotic and antisocial enough to keep most people at bay, but he wasn't stupid. He cherished the free-dom of his wilderness lifestyle too much to risk going to prison over a willful, wildly misguided, and passionate girl. No, I need not worry about being whacked on the back of the head, hav-ing my face shoved beneath the water, or being reduced to kin-dling in a major crack-up. I could just as easily go under from hypothermia or exhaustion.

Gaining strength as it rose, the sun wicked water from my shirt and pants, dried my hair, and eased my shivering. Gain-ing confidence, I began to relax and enjoy myself. I paddled with unrestrained enthusiasm in hopes that Bill would con-sider me still worthy. Perhaps I could still prove that I was indispensable. I needed to convince him that he couldn't live without a woman who fed the horses, milked the goats, made butter and cheese, canned produce, split kindling, cooked on a wood stove, washed clothes in the river, rode bareback, beaded his moccasins, snowshoed eight miles for the mail, *and* pad-dled a canoe with aplomb. I began to consider the possibility that under his stoic, hard-ass attitude there might be a heart that could forgive, if not forget, my purposeful unfaithfulness. That line of thinking stiffened my spine. Why should I be apol-ogetic? Bill refused to be married, and I was still a single woman. He took no responsibility for me beyond the neces-

sities of daily life. Maybe he should examine how his own
womanizing tendencies had fostered my first exploration of
forbidden sexual territory.

"Heads up," Bill said. I had been staring at my paddle parting the pewter water and looked up in time to notice that the
river in front of us was gone, replaced by an expanse of air
emitting a dull, low-throated, ominous growl. "Paddle as long
as you can," he shouted. "Then hang on."

The broad cascade boasted boulders at the bottom of the
small fall. It wasn't that much of a drop, but when the front of
the canoe spilled over the lip, I jammed the paddle between my
thighs and clutched the bow with both hands as bilious nausea
crawled from my stomach to lodge in my gullet. No scream
this time, only an effort to try to breathe around the sickening
obstruction. Bill, however, whooped like a bronc rider making
the eight-second whistle. What was it about adrenalin that
turned him on, made him delirious and joyful? The bow
smacked down between two rocks, bounced beach-ball easy a
time or two, then settled with a stern shake before sliding into
calm water. I picked up my paddle with trembling hands, sliced
the pool a few times, then turned around to sneak a peek at Bill.

He sat upright, his back lodgepole straight, paddle balanced
across his lap, arms down, fingertips trailing in the water, face
upturned to intermingled splashes of sun and cottonwood
shadow. Was he praying? What was that beatific look? Splendor?
Rapture? Certainly an altered state of consciousness. Not an
expression I had ever seen before, not even after a sensual lovemaking session. He opened his eyes and lowered his head until
his hazel orbs met mine of dark chocolate. Little lightning bolts
shot between us, an electric chemistry concocted of attraction,
need, longing, and lust. But not love. No, it couldn't be love,
because behind the dancing sparks there still surged a snaking
current of hot-wire anger. I blinked first—then turned away.

The river rolled under us, the canoe riding high, light, and
airy. Pulsing with spring intensity, the sunshine made it hard to

believe I had been bitter cold just an hour before. I wanted to
stay in this perfect moment, savor the spectacular view that
shifted from the high peaks in Glacier National Park to thick
stands of dog-hair pine, but snapshots flipped before my
mind's eye: Jim helping a newborn spotted filly find her legs.
Jim bringing me magazines to read. Jim humming and whistling as we worked to ready the garden for planting. Jim staring
at me from across the yard while I showered under the solar-
heated outdoor water tank. Jim . . .

"Look alive," Bill said. "It's a long series, and I'll need help."
The notion that Bill—fierce, stubborn, independent—needed
help with anything was new. I jerked upright, readied my paddle, and paid attention. The river spread out in a series of fan-
ned skirts, each one creating the illusion of being smooth as
silk. Far ahead, the channel narrowed, and a ruffle of white lace
appeared at her throat, from which a boisterous reverberation
echoed.

"That's where we're headed," Bill said. "Third chute from
the left. Don't think. Don't second-guess. Just keep paddling.
Remember to breathe."

I nodded and tried to grip my paddle in a way that didn't
irritate the red beginnings of blisters. I took my wet gloves off.
Put them on. Took them off and jammed them into my pants
pocket. We fast-slid toward the sloping channel Bill had chosen. Even over the roar of the water, I could hear him breathing. The strain of forcing the canoe into the proper presenta-
tion for the rapid burned in his lungs. I paddled left, paddled
right, paddled without even knowing which side I was leaning
to, my knees spread wide to brace against the canoe's drenched
shoulders. Then there was no river, no stillness, no pools, no
wavelets lapping gravel bars, no long, calm stretch mirroring
cloud reflections. There was nothing but water. Everywhere.
Plumes, geysers, sucking whirlpools. Boulders appeared out
of nowhere, then disappeared beneath waves and surges. The
canoe rammed one rock, slammed into another, her shellacked

cedar strips groaning under the pressure. Every thought I'd had about staying safe vanished. I quit paddling and focused on shoving us away from dripping walls of stone. The agitation of being tossed around and around felt like being inside an immense washing machine set on heavy load/cold water. I heard nothing from Bill—no commands, no directions. I feared that he had been dumped overboard, and I whipped my head around just long enough to see him bent low, his face a grimace of concentration. No sooner had we cleared one sliding rapid descent than another one dropped before us.

Miles later, I knew nothing except that I had forgotten to breathe, and I ached all over. My hands felt like ground hamburger, my mind was torn to tatters, but in my heart a gigantic love for the river stirred. Shimmering golden blue-green light over the dark undercurrent, the river finally ran out of energy and wound down. The water's voice switched to a soothing lullaby that rocked the canoe as a mother rocks a child to sleep. Bill pulled into deep water by a cut bank, saying, "Grab hold," and I reached out to snag the overhanging limbs of a willow with pale green leaves and fuzzy buds. As I held us in place, he bailed out the cargo of murky water. "No more surprises," he said. "It's an easy run from here. Several more miles."

He pulled strips of elk jerky from the pack and gave me several along with a handful of dried cherries. We drifted, chewing in silence, dipping a tin cup to drink where a side creek emptied clear water over gravel. Clean-sheet fresh, an afternoon breeze picked up, spanking my already sun-pink face. The river had eaten Bill's anger, chugged down my fear. There was so much to say, and no way to say it. Letting silence soothe the raw unspoken edge of everything that had happened, I decided not to say a word until we reached Polebridge.

I spotted Bill's green stock truck with the boat rack before I noticed Jim leaning against a tree watching our approach. Bill angled the canoe to shore, and I stumbled into knee-deep water, taking the bowline along. When he stepped up beside me, pushing long hair out of his eyes and resetting his beaded headband, I asked again, "Bill?"

"Stop," he said, taking a long-drawn inhalation of breath. "There's nothing to say. You either love this way of life or you don't. You'll either stay or you won't." He rough-whacked me on the rump, pulled the canoe to high ground, and walked toward Jim with his hand outstretched, saying, "Thanks for coming to pick us up."

I tried not to cry. For weeks, for months, I had held it all back. But now, unbidden and unwanted, hot-sharp tears burned my eyes, and a pained mewling cry emerged from my enforced silence. I could not focus on the two men talking side by side. Not knowing which direction to go, the world a blur, I walked in a circle, then turned back to the water, knelt, and splashed my face. The river, sighing over stone and sand, whispered, "stay . . . stay . . . stay . . . " I understood, for perhaps the first time, that my insane reason for staying with Bill had little to do with loving him. It had to do with my determination to stay in a landscape I had come to love more than myself.

Death in Autumn

In fall 1977, Bill's mother, Catherine, brought his younger
brother, Bob, from Florida for a visit. Although Bob was in his
thirties, he walked and talked and ate like a zombie-child due
to the heavy sedation of antipsychotic drugs. Catherine had
pulled every string she had to find a way to get Bob released
from the institution where he had been sentenced to remain
until his illness could be brought under control. She and Bill
both thought that time away from people, the stress of trying
to find a job, the complications of city life, and the demands of
trying to appear normal might give Bob a chance to find himself again. Was he suffering from bipolar disorder, paranoia,
schizophrenia, psychotic delusions? No one knew. All we did
know was that he had jumped on the Anita Bryant bandwagon
in her campaign against homosexuality and was arrested while
trying to use a hypodermic needle to inject air into the arm
vein of a drugged-out homeless person asleep on a Jacksonville
street—that and the fact that his mother had once found him
in the middle of the night in the garage eating a box of rat poi-

139

son. Bob was tall, handsome, well educated, well read, a brilliant philosopher and conversationalist, but I am not ashamed
to say that he frightened me.

The second morning of Bob and Catherine's visit, I walked
in from doing the morning milking to find Catherine sitting
calmly on the couch reading and Bob standing by the living
room table holding one of Bill's pistols. I set down the milk
bucket and went back outside, where Bill was fleshing a deer
hide, and said, "He's got a gun." Bill went in and talked to his
brother, explaining that all the weapons were loaded and that
he needed to be careful. Bob nodded his understanding. Later,
while Bob was napping, the three of us sat in the kitchen and
discussed the situation. Bill said, "Hell, we can't put away every
rifle and pistol. If I do that, I would need to hide every knife
and piece of rope, not to mention that there's a river right outside the door." He and his mother agreed that we would try for
normalcy and calm, trusting that a loving, supportive environment would help Bob heal and find his way.

When the weather turned colder and winter snow threatened, Catherine knew she had to leave to get downcountry,
catch a plane, and fly back to Florida, where her husband and
the boys' father, Andrew, was anticipating her return. We had a
tearful farewell at the border, where a ride waited to take her
into town. Bill, astride his stud, was in good spirits. Bob,
astride the gelding, had been doing well, even joining in daily
conversations and activities as he was weaned gradually from
the overload of prescription drugs. Bill hoped that Bob would
soon be able to pitch in with chores like splitting wood and
feeding hay, simple tasks that would reconnect him with the
value of a job well done, something he might feel good about.
Perhaps contact with the animals, both wild and domestic,
would help him find his primal desire to survive and be content with little things, like sunshine, fresh air, good food, and a
warm bed. Bill knew firsthand how those things could help
save a man from self-destruction.

We had butchered the hog, Brother Woink, weeks earlier, and the hams and bacons grew fragrant and gold in the smokehouse. The already smoked sausages curled inside a five-gallon crock covered with lard. The only task left was to render and can the leaf lard for baking and cooking. Bill and I spent the morning cutting the slippery slabs of fat into small pieces and sliding them off into the vat of bubbling grease. When one batch of cracklings turned light brown, we scooped them out with a slotted spoon to cool on stacks of newspaper. What we didn't eat would go to the chickens, cats, and dog. After breakfast, Bob had settled on the couch to read but had fallen asleep. His snores created a grating melodic accompaniment to our work.

When the last of the hot grease had been ladled into clean, dry gallon jars and sealed, Bill and I decided to walk up to the border to say good-bye to the station attendant, Evans, and his wife, Irene, who were leaving for the winter. We walked out into the rarefied fall air, leaving Bob snoozing in the warm cabin. When we returned, visitors were waiting for us out by the barn. Jim and a friend had tags for the next hunting season and had driven up from Kalispell to scout for elk.

Suppertime was close. I had chores to do and a meal to fix for five, so I hurried into the cabin. It was cold. The fires were out. Bob was not on the couch. I assumed he had gone upstairs. Rustling around, I built a fire, then pulled leftovers from the cooler cupboard behind the couch. I noticed that Bill's .30-.30 was gone. In its place was a folded piece of paper. I didn't touch it. I went upstairs to find Bob. He wasn't there. I searched the two rooms, even looking under the beds. It took me the longest time to pick up the note on the back of the couch and walk outside.

"What?" Bill said when I handed it to him.

"Your rifle's gone," I said. "I found this."

"Bob?"

"Not here," I said. "At least not in the house."

Bill read the note and crushed it into his shirt pocket. He explained to Jim and his friend about Bob and asked them to help with a search of all the vacant cabins, barns, and other outbuildings. All three had been in Vietnam. None seemed afraid.

I stood there helpless. "Go on," Bill said. "Fix supper. Do the milking. I'll go tell Evans to wait in case we don't find him. He has a radio."

In the root cellar, by the late dim light coming down the stairs from the open door above, I searched for a jar of pickles. The glass was cold and hard in my hand. When I turned to walk back up the stairs, I found Jim waiting for me. He took the half-gallon jar and the lamp.

"Anything?" I asked.

"No," he said. "Are you all right?"

"No," I said. "But if I start crying I won't stop, and that won't do a thing except make Bill mad. What do I do, Jim? What do I do to help?"

"There's nothing you can do." He set the glass jar and burning lamp on the wood steps. "But wait."

Jim gathered me into his arms and pressed me to his flannel-warm chest. We stood, my cheek to his heart, his chin on the top of my head, until his compassion settled me down.

The four of us ate in near-silence. Bill had ridden across the meadow to some other abandoned summer cabins. Evans had put the call out for search and rescue on his radio, and then headed for town with his wife. At dark Jim asked if they should stay, but Bill told them there was nothing they could do, to go on, so they pulled out as well. Bill sat at the table as I did dishes. Then he said, "I'm going out to look some more." He never came home. He rode all night, searching.

He was still gone the next morning when the bloodhounds came. The handler asked me some questions, requested an article of Bob's clothing, told me to be sure not to touch it with my hands. I took a hemostat from a drawer, walked upstairs, clam-

ped it onto one of Bob's dirty t-shirts, and brought it down to
the dogs. They ran crying into the morning, many men following. Vehicles crowded the yard; people swarmed and shouted.
Bill returned. The Appy stud stood head down, crusted with
sweat. Bill would not come in to rest. He would not drink the
cup of tea I brought to him.

Our friends Ray and Liz had heard the news flashing back
and forth on the CB. Ray stood outside with Bill. Liz held
my hand across the kitchen table. It was hard to talk because
there didn't seem to be anything to say. Hours went by. Men
returned with the word that they had found nothing. Someone,
though, had called in to say they had heard a gunshot downriver late the previous afternoon. The search shifted directions.

Then one lone man trudged in. The muffled sound of his
report made the rounds from mouth to mouth. The officer in
charge came to talk to Bill, and a handful of men left to retrieve
the body. Bob had crawled under a cabin downriver. He had
needed only one shot to end his life. The only thing I saw was
the brown rubber bag in the back of a pickup truck. Liz stayed
with me while Ray drove Bill to Polebridge to call his parents.
When they returned, Bill thanked our friends and sent them on
their way. In the quiet that occurred after everyone's departure,
the wind coming out of Canada howled, bringing snow. Bill
refused to talk. He would not accept a kind word or a gesture
of comfort. When I tried to hug him, he shoved me away.

In slow motion, he gathered gear and warm clothing. I followed him out to the barn, asking, "Where are you going?" but
he wouldn't answer. He saddled one horse and packed another.
He rode away into the night, heading north, the dog following
him. I was left alone with only the fire for company, with a
ghost prowling outside, wailing around the corners of the
cabin. I didn't go upstairs to bed. I sat in a chair wearing my
coat, with a lamp burning low at the window.

A horrible wind rose. The pines screamed in bending gyra-
tions. Flapping tin on the roof ripped loose and smashed into

the river. The goats careened past the cabin, bells clanging.
Even the chickens locked in their henhouse set up a raucous
clucking. A gray dawn illuminated the wreckage. The rooster
didn't even bother to crow. Trees were down everywhere. The
rabbit cages broken to the ground. Fences crushed. I had not
slept, but still there were chores to do. I milked the nervous
goats and forked out hay. I found the frightened rabbits and
tucked them into the one solid cage. I opened the door for the
chickens, but they didn't even want to venture outside. The
river whined with an overload of debris.

Bill rode in and unsaddled his horses. He didn't want anything to eat. He refused to speak. We were out cutting trees off
fences when Irene drove in. She said she would take us to town
to attend to details. Bill needed to call his parents again. He
needed to go to the funeral home to make arrangements for
Bob's body. The sheriff wanted to speak with him. We could
stay with her and Evans. She would fix us a good supper.

Bill accepted her offer, but clearly going to town did not help
him in any way. We waited in the car while he spoke with the
sheriff and returned with the rifle Bob had used to kill himself.
He waited in the car while Irene and I went into the funeral
home to pick up Bob's sullied clothes. Catherine had called the
funeral home from Florida and asked them to cremate Bob's
body and send the ashes to her and Andrew in Jacksonville.
While Irene fixed supper, Bill tried to talk to his parents on the
phone. Tears ran down his cheeks and into his beard. I placed
the palm of my hand on his rigid back to let him know I was
there for him. When he hung up the phone, I tried to embrace
him, to let him know I loved him. He glared at me, his eyes full
of blame and anger. "If you'd been kinder to him, perhaps this
would not have happened." He walked into the other room and
stared out the window.

Irene took me by the hand and led me into the basement,
where she took the belt from Bob's pants and put them and the
bloody shirt, t-shirt, underwear, and socks into the washer.

"He'll get over it," she said. "It may just take some time." She put Bob's shoes and belt into a clean paper sack.

I knew better. I knew Bill would never get over another violation of his heart. If I was to blame, then that would have to be the burden I would carry along with all the others. I followed Irene back upstairs. I stood at the sink and peeled potatoes. I was very careful to remove every strip of greenish skin and to cut out each dark pit of an eye.

∾

With the New Year came a letter from the absentee landowner saying that we had to leave in the spring. They gave Bill a deadline. On official-looking stationery, the reasons given were many but trivial: the goats were noisy and smelly, the piles of hair from fleshed deer and elk hides were unsightly, the free-ranging horses ate too much grass, there had been complaints from park rangers and Game and Fish officials. But we knew the real reason was Bob's death. Bill's twelve-year caretaker's residency in the cabin above the river was over. He was sullen and angry, full of hatred, agony, and stoic silence. My insecurity and fears didn't help mend the rents and tears in the tenuous, fragile, and complicated spider web of our conflicted love.

The time came to pull out. After weeks of butchering and canning chickens, goats, and rabbits, after sorting and burning belongings for days, I had grown tough enough to shoot the pup I couldn't find a home for, hardened enough to shoot the cats no one wanted. It seemed cold-hearted, but a kinder fate than leaving them to starve. At least I knew that the animals I had loved were safe in the earth.

Bill and I wandered in the one-ton stock truck with the horses and the hound, living in a tepee camp wherever we could find a flat, grassy place to lay our beds. By summer's end we had not found a new place to call home. I had not had a period since we had left the Northfork, nor had I seen a doctor. Bill's simmering bitterness kept me from saying anything.

Instead, when we were close enough to a city for me to find an airport, I asked him to drive me there. I had had enough sense to squirrel away a couple hundred dollars, and I had packed a few important things in one small suitcase. When Bill pulled up in front of "Departures" at the Denver International Airport, he reached across me and shoved open my door. When I started to talk to him, to try to say good-bye, he turned his head away. When I didn't move, he raised his leg, put his foot against my thigh, and shoved. I slid out, walked to the rear of the truck for my suitcase, then headed into the terminal. I did not look back. Nor did I cry.

Sorting Pairs

When Bill left me at the airport, I knew that I was going home to Chicago to see my family. I didn't know that I would work in an airless factory for three months to save enough money to return to the West. While Bill holed up for the winter with Kyote and the horses at a remote homestead in Canada, I spent the long cold months in Kalispell working for the community college. Come spring, I bought a used station wagon and headed to Bozeman for nine months at Montana State University to finish the undergraduate degree in English literature that I had abandoned years before. Wherever I went, Bill's letters found me. Although I wrote back, I was not ready to return. After graduating, I answered an ad for a housekeeper on the IX Ranch in the Bear Paw Mountains outside Havre, Montana. Keen to be horseback again, I headed north to learn about cows and cowboys.

The wind blew sharp for August. To the west, Ryan Butte looked hunched and cold under a weight of clouds. Sixty miles south, the flat top of Square Butte was vaguely visible beyond the Missouri River Breaks. Four of us, hugged close in the pickup cab, bounced along a narrow track that led across the Mud Lake field, six thousand acres of rangeland that was part of the IX Ranch in north-central Montana. A trailer full of saddled Quarter horses rattled along behind.

In the cab, the men stayed quiet. The foreman, Rusty, concentrated on keeping the truck and trailer on level ground. Another hand, Rich, pulled a tin of Copenhagen from his back pocket, took a pinch, and passed it to Eugen (pronounced *OY-gen*), politely smiling as he passed me by. A half-hour later, the truck crawled to a stop near a windmill water tank and everyone piled out, stretching cramped limbs. The rising sun colored the sky with silver and magenta light.

The horses unloaded without trouble. The men zipped on chaps, buckled on spurs, searched for gloves, and tied on slickers. Rusty considerately checked my cinch, helped me mount, and adjusted my stirrups. "Rich, Laurie," he said, swinging onto his bay gelding, "ride west, push them off the buttes. Eugen and I will cover here." He snugged down his hat and loped away.

Rich and I circled west, our horses trotting briskly in unison, picking their way around rocks and clumps of sage. When we reached the fringe of buttes, Rich told me to check the coulees for cow-calf pairs, then galloped off on his own. I waited for a moment, pondering the fact that I had never pushed cows before, but the mare anxiously bobbed her head and pawed the ground. So I turned away from the sun, heeled her into a trot, and headed up the first draw.

Since June I had cooked meals and managed the household at Eagle Creek, one of the five IX ranches that lay in the Bear Paw Mountains south of the Rocky Boy Indian Reservation.

Today, for the first time, the men had invited me to ride along as they worked the cattle. I was well aware that I was a "greenhorn," but I had already learned that open eyes and a closed mouth would be my best advantage with men who did their work with little or no conversation.

Flushing a jackrabbit, the mare snorted and sidestepped without warning; but she instantly regained her measured trot and cocked her ears forward. There: at the top of the draw, several pairs grazed on short-stemmed bunchgrass. My inexperience mattered little, for the mare went to work, and I was along for the lesson. The sight of the horse alerted the pairs, sending the calves skittering to their mamas. The mare circled wide, coming in behind the cows, which began to move, bawling, gathering into a bunch and ambling down the draw. Smiling at the apparent ease of the operation, I turned up the next coulee.

On the crest of a high ridge, I spotted the other hands in the distance. Cattle moved in from all directions, collecting into one large brown-and-white herd on the pale green-gold flats below. The few head I pushed jogged to join the bunch. Above the droning call of the cattle, I heard the occasional yell of a rider.

By eight o'clock I had pushed close to thirty head, seen a small herd of antelope in flight, startled half a dozen sharp-tailed grouse, and checked the last draw on the west side. The mare had worked up a light sweat, and my legs ached. But the morning had just begun. The cattle, some three hundred pairs, were strung out for over a mile, all heading north. Rich and Rusty rode point and swing to check the direction of the lead cows and keep the herd from wandering. Eugen and I rode drag, pushing the cows from behind and coaxing stragglers.

When the tail end of the herd caught up with the lead cows near the Stage Cabin field, the day was warmer, and seven other IX hands had appeared. Altogether I counted twelve riders, including Art Roth, owner and operator of the IX. At first, everything seemed to be a welter of chaotic confusion, with horses, riders, and cattle milling around on the wide plain. Then Art designated a position for each rider, and the process of sorting pairs began.

Four of us held the herd, keeping the cattle contained and retrieving any strays that broke away. Art's sons, Steve and Rich, and two of the foremen, Rusty and Bill, worked in two-man cutting teams. The remaining riders moved the sorted pairs to different pastures and kept a tally on the number of cattle worked. In a precise, time-consuming dance of horses and men, the cattle were cut three ways: steer pairs moved to the Ryan field would be marketed in the fall; heifer pairs moved to the Schoolhouse field would be kept as possible replacement stock; dry cows and orphaned or unbranded calves moved to the Stage Cabin field would be worked in the afternoon. Throughout the action, Art carefully examined the cattle, picking out any ill or injured animals.

I sat my mare facing the herd, amazed by the alertness of the horses as they worked. Not only were the men constantly aware, but the horses were as well, responding immediately to any movement of the cattle. Even as the mare dozed with half-closed eyes, she had one ear cocked forward and one tilted back in readiness. A cow or calf occasionally bolted from the herd, and one of the men galloped off in pursuit, his horse following every dodge of the stray. The morning passed, measured only by the height of the sun and the rich mix of dust in the air.

Near noon, Art called in the riders with a wave of his hand and a holler. With two hundred–plus pairs sorted, we released the remaining unpaired cows and calves to be worked the following day. The job over for the moment, the men began to joke and laugh, talking over the events of the morning. Someone asked me, "How ya doin'?" Windblown and dry-throated, all I could do was nod okay and smile.

The whole crew trailed over to the Stage Cabin field for lunch. After loosening cinches and removing bridles, the men turned the horses into a pole corral and went right to work on sack lunches of sandwiches, fruit, cake, and iced tea. Before long, amid grunts and groans of satisfaction, they stretched out in the patchy shade of trucks and trailers for an hour's rest. Except for an infrequent snore or the dim bawl of a calf, the day stayed silent and hot.

In the afternoon, half the men returned to fencing and irrigating, while the rest stayed on to work the unbranded calves missed during the spring roundup. Eugen gathered and corralled the pairs. Bill set up a portable propane torch. Art sharpened his pocketknife. Steve mixed up a bucket of disinfectant. Rusty filled a syringe with vaccine. Rich sat astride his gelding, coiling his lariat. I stood to one side trying to stay out of the way.

Eugen swung open the gate, and Rich rode into the midst of the milling cattle, swinging a loop slowly over his head. A second later, with an accurate flip of his wrist, he settled the loop under a tiny pair of hooves, jerked the slack, dallied the rope around the horn, and exited the corral dragging a bull calf by its heels. Without delay, Steve and Rusty grabbed the head and heels, stretching out the calf on its right side. Art stepped in and castrated the calf with one quick motion, flung the testicles aside, turned for the hot iron, and seared three even lines into the hide, forming the IX brand. In the meantime, Bill cut out the horn buds and marked an ear, while Eugen injected vaccine into the loose fold of skin under the left foreleg. Released, the dazed calf scrambled to his feet and dashed away as Rich hauled in another.

The number of cattle in the corral dwindled to a handful of dry cows and a dozen orphan calves. With a great deal of shouting and shoving, the men ran the animals into a loading pen, up a chute, and onto a stock truck. They cornered the orphans and manhandled them into a trailer. "Guess that's it," Art commented, and everyone pitched in to clean up, pack the gear, and load the horses.

Way past four in the afternoon, the long line of trucks and trailers crept out of the Stage Cabin field and headed for home. Ours was the last vehicle to leave, and Rusty pulled over while Eugen hopped out to wrestle the wire gate closed. Once on the main road, the men resumed their quiet demeanor, the rattle of the trailer and the ping of loose gravel under the truck taking the place of conversation.

At Eagle Creek, Rusty stopped to let me off and asked, "Wanna ride tomorrow?"

"Sure," I answered without hesitation.

"Leaving at six," he added and pulled away.

I waved my thanks and walked stiffly toward the house. Sore and tired, my face sunburned, my hair caked with dust, I had survived the initiation ritual of open space, clean air, a good horse, hard work, and the camaraderie of kind and quiet men.

∾

By the end of September, I had harvested the garden and frozen and canned all the produce, plus picked the last of the berries and gathered the windfall apples to make jams and jellies. Also, thanks to Art and the boys, I had turned into a good hand with a saddle horse, and I had learned how to tell a steer from a heifer. Art and his wife, Audrey, offered me a full-time job and urged me to stay on at the IX over the winter.

While I had come to love their close-knit family and the haunting, wind-battered buttes, I longed for the untamed life I once lived on the Northfork. Despite Bill's caustic admonition in a recent missive that "the only thing dumber than a cow is a cowboy," and Audrey's motherly warnings about going back to a difficult relationship, I was determined to return to a landscape with fewer people and no traffic. I yearned for the close connection to and daily challenge of life on the land. The only way I knew to return to the wild was to return to Bill.

I sent the precious dollars I had earned and hoarded over the summer to pay off my student loans. I cleaned my room at the top of the stairs over the kitchen and packed my few belongings in my battered station wagon. Twenty-six years old and single, I had a degree in English literature and a letter of recommendation from one of Montana's top-notch cattle outfits. Still, the only thing I wanted was an unpopulated and unspoiled landscape. Bill was waiting for me in a cabin on the edge of Glacier National Park. Kyote, Jubilee, Jere, and the Appy stud, War Eagle, waited, too, along with a new milk doe and her kids. I hit the highway and headed farther west.

Exhaustion and nervousness strained my less than joyous homecoming. How had I forgotten how dicey the days could be depending on Bill's moods? Somberness and discontent soon snuffed out the radiant flame of being together again. In the space of a year, we moved from the ancient pack rat–infested cabin near West Glacier to a partially finished lodge in the Bitterroot Mountains near Lost Trail Pass. Before real winter closed the roads, we pulled out again, looking for wilder country. Bill needed to be beyond the reach of telephones, electricity, highway traffic, and people to maintain any kind of balance. I needed to cling to the belief that love and loyalty could cure our ills.

We found sanctuary at Snook's place.

Snook's Place

Bill and I pulled into Snook Moore's 160-acre ranch at the junction of Teepee Creek and Tosi Creek in the Upper Green River Valley west of the Bridger Wilderness of Wyoming in late October of 1981. The three horses stood tied nose to tail in the back of Bill's one-ton stock truck. The bulk of our worldly belongings were jammed into a homemade trailer and my ten-year-old Vista Cruiser station wagon.

When I showed up on the Moore ranch as Bill's female friend, Snook was a gentleman of the highest order. He had incredibly blue twinkling eyes and a big square jaw, and was on the verge of turning sixty-five. He tipped his battered Stetson to me and helped me carry our belongings into the two-room cabin that would serve as our home. With the extreme politeness born of backcountry living, he invited us to dinner. Then, when we declined, saying it should be us serving him, and invited him to our table, he insisted on bringing the elk steaks and sourdough biscuits.

The following day I showed up on Snook's doorstep, ready and willing to help with chores to pay back his kindness of giving us a home. A foot of snow already covered the rugged landscape, and he had stock that needed to be fed. The first thing Snook taught me was how to choke up on a pitchfork handle and how to pace my "shoveling" of hay onto the rack of the horse-drawn feed sled. "It will do you no good to burn yourself out," he said. "Pace is everything. Slow and steady gets you there every time."

It never failed, daybreak long into evening, that Snook did his work joyfully, humming a tune, whistling a string of harmonious notes, or telling me a litany of stories. His beloved lodge, painstakingly crafted log by log four decades earlier, had burned to the ground the year before. He had lost all of his personal belongings save his rifle, his sleeping bag, a jar of sourdough, and a fork. Still, while his wife, Evalyn, wintered in California with her daughter, he holed up happily in one of his guest cabins and continued to live his life fully, without sadness, without bitterness.

We became close friends immediately and knew one another's life stories within a week. He listened to my complaints and problems like a grandfather and tendered advice like a sage. Together we shoveled snow off the cabin roofs, split wood, parceled out the carefully hoarded hay to the horses and milk cows, and fed the chickens. Mornings, Snook fixed breakfast at his cabin. Evenings, I fixed supper at mine. We shared the dish chores. During the long afternoons when I tired of doing beadwork, writing letters, or reading, I trekked up to Snook's place for more stories. I liked to watch him sew buttons on his worn shirts, darn his holey socks, or tie an indescribably beautiful orange fly that he would use to cast for California golden trout in the Wind River Mountains come summer.

Busy tanning and smoking hides and working on his engravings, Bill disappeared into the background. He said nothing, but he watched my blossoming relationship with Snook like a fierce hawk. He had made one room of the two-room cabin into his private sanctuary, with a single bed, the wood heat stove, and a worktable under the window for good light. I was to knock before entering. My room contained a log frame double bed, the wood cook stove, a cupboard for dishes, and a table with two chairs. Bill rarely visited my side of the cabin except for meals, and I was never invited to visit him. The grudge he bore me for my earlier infidelity sat on his shoulder like a chopping block. He did not believe in forgiveness or talking things out. He did not believe in getting mad. He believed in getting even.

During December and January, blizzards rolled in one after the other, piling the drifts deep, burying my old car and Snook's 1954 pickup truck under four feet of snow. Coyotes sang nightly. Moose crowded the creek bottoms in search of willows. When Bill and I lived on the Northfork, elk and deer were a common sight, but moose less so. We considered seeing a moose a special event. They were shy and solitary creatures, and we never feared them. At Snook's, however, when the weather started out fierce and never let up, the snow deepened until fences disappeared and narrow trails marked our coming and goings from the cabin to the root cellar, outhouse, and barns. Snook warned us early on about the moose: "They're dangerous. Stay out of their way." We grinned and nodded, not fully heeding his warning.

One dawn, Bill, on his way to the outhouse at first light, came back to the cabin and said, "Come look." We crept outside and eased around the corner of the building. Fifty feet away lay a cow and calf moose on the sheltered lee side of another cabin. We ducked back, talked in whispered voices, and then peered around for a second look. The cow sprang and charged, her front feet flailing the air. We barely made it back inside. Wham! Wham! She struck the hastily slammed door.

I snowshoed out one afternoon to pack our mail trail and mark it with willow sticks. The dogs bounded off after something dark on a nearby ridge. I whistled them back and ordered them to stay while I went to investigate. I found a starving calf moose with both front legs shot off at the knees. Even so, the brave creature made its pitiful stand, with hackles raised and tongue wagging. From the tracks, I could see where the cow had returned again and again, urging her fatally crippled youngster to follow her south. With the nearest phone miles away and only a pocketknife in my pack, my sole choice was to snowshoe home to alert Snook or Bill to get a rifle. The calf became dog food. Thereafter, when I skied downcountry for exercise in the afternoons, my heart beat faster and my palms grew sweaty as I hurried through the willow bottoms, anxious to reach higher ground where I could spot lurking moose.

For Snook it was the same old story. When the snows got deep, the moose traveled the bottoms looking for feed. They became ornery and belligerent, and challenged anyone or anything in their path. We walked the skinny trails with more caution. Snook took to packing his .45 when he hiked in the dark from his cabin to ours for supper. By lamplight and the warm glow of the wood stove, he told us story after story of confrontation: Sawing wood near his garage one fall, he felt, rather than saw, a moose charge. He wheeled, his chain saw buzzing in defense, and backed into the building, kicking the door shut. He was left stranded until the moose tired of beating up the building and left . . . Coming down the packed trail between the cabins, he and his dog, aptly named Moose, were charged and struck. The large dog leapt and grabbed for the moose's nose while Snook made his escape. The moose went down, its air choked off, and Snook had to pry his dog's jaws open to loosen its hold . . . A group of snowmachiners on a groomed trail up Tosi Creek were winding their way through thick willows when the last one in line slowed for a turn. A moose charged, knocked the woman from her machine, trampled her, and battered the snowmobile; only the deep snow and her thick winter clothing saved her from serious injury.

All through January, February, March, and April, the moose hung on the edge of Snook's feedground hoping for a bit of the precious hay we doled out with care to the horse herd. Twenty-two dead moose littered the creek bottoms when the snow began to melt off. Bill reported lion tracks around a carcass near the falls.

Snook had counted the days until spring, marking them off on his calendar and hoping his hay would last. I followed him along the trail he had tramped to the corrals, and his three constant-companion dogs followed me. After caring for the chickens, we harnessed the winter work team, Nugget and Bally. Nugget was a Quarter horse–Percheron cross, and Bally, with his salad-plate-sized feet, was part Shire, part Belgian. Together the geldings added up to three thousand pounds of horsepower, capable of pulling quite a load. Snook hitched them to his handmade sled, and we trundled off across the windblown fields to feed. Twelve-foot-high log cribs held Snook's hay, which he had laboriously cut, raked, loaded, and stacked the previous summer with horse-drawn equipment. We loaded the precious hay onto the sled with care, pitching on about a thousand pounds a day to feed the herd of seventeen horses and a couple of Hereford cows. I had fed hay to animals on and off for seven years and had cleaned many barns with pitchforks, but I had a whole lot to learn about arm muscle and patience. For the first two months, I never even attempted to help harness. I would stand and watch Snook and ask, "What's this? What's that?" He would answer: "Hames, post strap, collar, check rein, traces, belly band, quarter straps, britchin', tugs, post, tongue, single tree, double tree, bunk, bolster."

The complex maze of straps and buckles remained a puzzle to me until I asked Snook to show me how to use them, step by step. "It's easy," he said. "First the collar; pull her snug. Grab the harness by putting the left quarter strap on your right shoulder, then pick up a hame in each hand, swing'er up and over onto the horse's back. Adjust and fasten the hames around the collar, straighten out the traces, pull the tail through the britchin', fasten the quarter straps and the belly band, and put on the bridle." And he was right. Once I had harnessed a hundred times, it became as easy as breathing.

After feeding, Snook often cut, peeled, and sharpened lodgepole posts in preparation for fence mending. He replaced broken corral poles, fixed gates, repaired wagon tongues. The evenings found him making mohair cinches, braiding eight-strand rawhide bosals, weaving horsehair saddle blankets, or building panniers. Evenings were also the times for more story-telling, and that's when I learned the details of Snook's life.

∾

Snook remembered taking an all-day ride when he was four with his father, uncle, and brother. They left their ranch on the Gros Ventre River, crossed Bear Cabin Creek, and traveled down Cow Creek to make a thirty-mile loop. That was his beginning as a horseman. He broke his first horse when he was twelve, and by the time he was fourteen, he was breaking horses regularly for ten dollars a head. That fourteenth year was also when Snook left home with the clothes on his back and his saddle horse. All winter he worked for his room and board at the Ben Seaton Ranch, went to school, and ran a trap line. The following spring, Snook had two sets of clothes, his horse, and sixty dollars, and he was on the move again.

That summer, Snook drove a four-horse grader for the county road crew and then went to work for cattle outfits on Spread Creek and Black Rock. The DC Bar Ranch hired him when he was sixteen, and for three years he worked cattle and rodeoed every Sunday. That weekly rodeo practice gave him the expertise he needed for his next job. At eighteen, Snook became one of the rough-string riders for the Green River

Cattle Association, which ran about ten thousand head of
Hereford cattle over an approximately hundred-square-mile
range. Riding broncs and keeping tabs on all those cows were
some of Snook's best times, regardless of the fact that all he had
to his name were his three horses and his bedroll.

Snook saved money and bought the ranch on Tosi Creek in
1937, when he decided to settle down and start an outfit of his
own. He had his same three horses, a new bride, Evalyn, and, as
he liked to say, "a pocket full of dreams." That first year he and
Evalyn lived in a one-room, sod-roofed log cabin, and they
spent the summer grubbing out sagebrush with hoes. The wild
hay flourished, and Snook started building the log cabins,
sheds, and barns using only a hand ax and a one-man crosscut
saw. When he needed help pulling the huge ridge timbers into
place, Fox, his sorrel saddle horse, filled the bill.

As the ranch grew, Snook took other jobs to earn the money
necessary to keep things running. He worked as a coal miner,
sawyer, and fence builder. He tended a prize herd of Angus
cattle for the Lumin Horse, Cattle, and Sheep Company. He
broke horses for the HC Cattle Company in California, near
where his sister lived. For nineteen years he also fed elk herds
for the Department of Game and Fish, and he often snowshoed
twenty-four miles daily between his ranch and the Green River
elk feedground. In time he began to breed and raise his own
horses—Arabian–Quarter horse crosses that produced the
tough, sturdy, and endurance-blooded horses he needed for
riding the steep, rocky mountains that surrounded his home.
Snook liked to say, "and I broke and trained every colt in the
herd."

The why and wherefore of breaking horses was simple to
Snook: he treated each horse as an individual and respected
its native intelligence. Figuring out and understanding each
horse's disposition became Snook's key. "Some horses learn
slow, some fast. It's patience that turns out a good, well-broke
horse."

Snook's rough-string days ended after he had surgery to replace his right hip joint when he was sixty-one. He said, "I never rides a bronc unless I have to," like the fall before I met him, when a brown gelding came unglued and so did Snook. Unconscious for a time, he suffered three broken ribs and a torn-up shoulder, but he caught the "brute" down the trail and rode back to the ranch. "I kept right on riding, too," he said, "every day, all fall, to finish out my hunts and pack in the meat."

A legend in his time, Snook was known primarily for his backwoods savvy and his uncanny hand with horses. More than that, however, he was a rare man in his unerring kindness and his ability to embrace and love most things. He was passionate about the land he walked on and rode over, that he fixed fence on, that he irrigated and hayed, and that he hunted and trapped. Devoted to his horses and dogs, he stayed fervent in his care for them. He knew them inside out, all their quirks and habits, their good qualities and their bad. He told me once that the saddest thing in a man's life was that he outlived his horses and his dogs. Snook cherished women and handled them with the same respect, tolerance, and appreciation with which he handled his horses. While still in his early twenties, he married a woman fifteen years his senior and remained faithfully devoted to her until his death. He was accepting, if not always totally understanding, of his fellow man. The only time I ever heard Snook Moore say an unfavorable thing was when he commented on the government in general, and the Forest Service in particular. Even so, that remark was just a laughing, passing putdown in the course of a shoot-the-bull conversation with some neighboring cowboys.

Perhaps kindness isn't that important a quality in a man. It never made Snook rich or even financially comfortable. He spent his entire life ranching 160 acres on a shoestring. Kindness never bought Snook any fame, either, but it made him a neighbor to everyone, and an enemy to none. Most of all, in my impressionable eyes, it made him a hero.

I had been in the West for eight years. With his silent, often rough and demanding demeanor, Bill had taught me how to be tough, uncomplaining, and alone in a fierce environment. With his quiet, unassuming, often humorous and kind manners, Snook Moore taught me what it meant to be a human being in connection with an unpredictable landscape.

Cabin Fever

That year at Snook's place wearied me. Winter seemed too much to handle. I had chosen to live with a hard man, who himself chose to live hand to mouth in rough environs. I had stuck it out with Bill on and off for most of my twenties, but in that tiny cabin on Snook's ranch, next to the rushing water of Teepee Creek, I realized that I had come to the end of my heavily used and much-frayed rope. No electricity. No plumbing. No telephone. No family and no friends, least of all any women to talk to. Mail came up once a week to a box at the end of the paved road twelve miles away—too far for me to go. Bill skied out on occasion, and sometimes an acquaintance of Snook's snowmachined in with the letters for a rare visit. The cabin, hand-built by Snook forty years earlier, sheltered us from the elements, but the ever-increasing snow still sifted in through the cracks between the logs and under the weathered windowsills. By early December, the snow had pulled a thigh-deep blanket over everything. Before spring, with six feet on the level, we snowshoed or walked on boot-packed trails over all the fences. I cooked and cleaned, washing clothes by hand with water carried from the creek and heated on the wood stove. I split and packed wood and helped Snook with the chores. But I remained discontent and restless.

In my off-hours I wrote letters and half-hearted lines of dismal poetry, or sat with my frozen feet flat against the hot sides of the cook stove and did beadwork. From the window I watched the grouchy starving moose wander the willow bottoms. They often pawed their beds on the lee side of the cabins and root cellar to escape the constant wind.

The hard work and tough weather took a toll. I slept alone on a sagging bed in the kitchen portion of our split-room cabin. Once the fire in the cook stove died down in the evening, the ever-present cold turned bitter. With caution, we hoarded the mountain of wood rounds we had cut and stacked in the fall. Despite curtains made from flour-sack towels, frost crusted the inside of the tiny panes of Depression-era glass in two small windows. Undressing for bed meant taking off buckskin pants and deer hair–lined moccasins. I kept on my long johns, undershirt, sweatshirt, and down vest. Donning cotton gloves and a knit cap, I crawled under the frigid covers to lie shivering beneath several wool blankets, an elk robe, and a bear hide, until my body heat warmed a spot and I could finally sleep.

I woke each morning to the hearty call of Snook's voice echoing across the silent landscape. I piled on pants and boots and coat, then broke the skim of ice on the indoor water bucket to splash my face clean and braided my long hair. Running uphill through the snow to Snook's already warm cabin made my blood race and readied me for another day. Nonetheless, I grew increasingly quiet, doing my house chores and outdoor work feeling morose. While the men traded stories about life in the mountains over each morning's stack of sourdough pancakes, I stared out the smoke-stained windows at the forbidding, desolate face of the Wind River peaks. I had heard of and read about cabin fever, but the illness wasn't within my realm of experience.

Both Bill and Snook, however, recognized what was wrong with me. They never said anything, but they took action on twin fronts to avert the approaching demons. Bill rigged up a propane light above the head of my bed as my Christmas gift. One evening after eating elk stew and cornbread with us, Snook pulled a Zane Grey novel out of the inside pocket of his coat, saying, "I thought you might like something to read."

I fell in love with Zane Grey. I gobbled up every delicious and indescribable word. Curled in bed, the tiny glow of propane light puddling on the pages of the first western fiction I had ever read, I greeted people I had never met and visited places I had never seen. I stayed up for hours and hours, worrying about wasting the precious propane, but unable to close the book until my eyes ran over with weary tears and would not stay open. The next morning I chattered like a magpie while Bill and Snook exchanged knowing glances. Snook showed me his bookshelf stuffed with a complete hardback collection of Zane Grey novels. He told me the story of meeting the famous writer on one of his forays to hunt and fish in the Pinedale area.

Night after night, I cuddled with Zane Grey's characters, listened to their stories, and empathized with their predicaments. I couldn't wait to discover how their lives turned out. My own troubles faded in the face of theirs. I was aware that my new addiction was a form of escapism, so I purposefully refused to allow myself to read during the sunlit hours. I did my daily chores with religious vigor and renewed enthusiasm because my reward would be another drunken evening of reading.

I finished a novel every second or third night. When I had read the sixty books that Snook had in his cabin, I read them all a second time. Bill dismissed Zane Grey as an eastern wannabe who had never lived in the West and only wrote fiction, but I was adamant in my appreciation for the writer. Zane Grey not only saved the day for me, he saved my sanity.

◞◟

While the snow still lay heavy on the land, Snook built a harness for Moose and taught me how to train a dog to pull a sled. Before the spring breakup, we snowshoed a long line uphill through the pine timber, setting traps for marten and ermine and sharing Snickers candy bars. When the ice went out, Bill took his canoe to hunt beaver on the Green River. I tagged along with Snook while he hunted beaver on Teepee and Tosi creeks. I carried my Browning .22 rifle, but I was such a notoriously bad shot that I had no confidence to try my hand at the task. Snook, in his usual understated, calm way, pointed out a muskrat sitting on a beaver house at the edge of a pond late one evening. The low light created shadows and dark angles in the last glow of the sun disappearing behind the ridge where we sat half-frozen and silent. "There," he said, "shoot that rat. If you miss, you'll miss clean." I took aim and squeezed off the shot, and the muskrat fell into the water like a rock. When Moose retrieved the rat and brought it to us, Snook raved about my marksmanship: I had drilled the little critter right through the eye. His praise meant more to me than any award or honor I had ever received.

During all the months that Snook and I worked together, I never heard him raise his voice or lose his temper. I never saw him mistreat an animal or say a critical or unkind thing about a person, place, or thing. Nearly forty years my senior, he treated me with genuine respect, honoring my intelligence while accepting my naïveté and appreciating my friendship.

With true spring came the task of repairing saddles and pack gear. Snook taught me how to stitch the leather seams and cut saddle strings. He invited me into the corral to watch him work around the horses' feet, showing me how to trim and how to shoe. I watched in horror as Snook and Bill tussled with a fancy-pants snorty mare until she ended up roped, thrown, and tied down so they could work on her feet.

"If you plan on being a real cowgirl," Bill said with caustic dryness, "you'd better learn to shoe your own horse."

"Maybe," Snook said with his usual even demeanor, "you ought to get the girl her own horse first."

Snook allowed me the use of a pair of nippers and a not-too-sharp rasp to work on his old palomino gelding, who politely held up one foot and then another for me and never jerked back or kicked. "Easy," he said. "Steady as you go. You can't learn it all in one day."

I joined Snook on the fences, the old team pulling the rattling wagon with supplies. I learned how to splice wire and pound posts. When we reached snowmelt ponds and creek crossings, Snook politely turned his back so I could wade out bootless and without britches to repair the breaks. Together we tore out beaver dams and set irrigation ditches to running. We cleaned corrals, shoveling the winter's worth of manure onto an old horse-drawn spreader that Snook drove with lazy nonchalance while I hung on the edge of the frame listening to his never-ending stories. Confident that I could handle the team on my own, Snook turned me loose with Bally and Nugget to drag the meadows. Sitting on a huge square-hewn log behind the horses, I rode waves of irrigation water, watching the manure float and drift into every nook and cranny of grassland.

When the high country began to open up, Snook and I rode. Without really instructing, he showed me how to sit my horse, how to hold the reins, how to communicate and reassure my mount, and how to eyeball each inch of landscape we passed through.

One day we rode downcountry to the Circle S Ranch to see if the people there had heard anything from Evalyn, who remained in California with her daughter. The snow was still hock-deep on the horses, and we picked our slow way from partially exposed sagebrush to leaning fence post across a still-white scene. At the ranch, Snook spoke on the phone like he was yelling across the room. He hung up and said, "She won't come until the snow's gone. Maybe another month." We enjoyed a great meal and some company, then tightened the cinches on the horses and retraced our twelve-mile route home again.

Later we rode way up Tosi Creek to see if the snow had left Snook's hunting camp intact. "Maybe come summer you'd like to join me and Heidi Sterns up here and learn to handle a pack string," he said. "You'll like Heidi. She's quiet like you. We'd give you your own horse and a little cash plus your tips from the dudes." Back at the cabin, I excitedly told Bill that Snook had offered me a summer job, and I couldn't wait for the snow to melt off. The following day, Snook took me aside and said that Bill had accused him of "wanting to get two young girls alone up in the high country" with him. Embarrassed, Snook said, "I never thought of such a thing. Heidi's worked for me for a couple years. I just wanted to give you the same chance." After that, Snook didn't come to our house for supper, nor did we go up the hill to his cabin for breakfast. He began going off to do his chores without me.

As the grass greened up, the sandhill cranes returned, the road dried out, and the wildflowers burst into bloom, Bill and Snook had a bad blowup. On the surface the argument seemed to be about the distribution of beaver pelts the two had collected together during the spring trapping season. Underneath lurked Bill's corrosive jealousy because Snook had invited me to spend the summer with him and Heidi taking out fly-fishing pack trips. Bill belligerently accused Snook of thievery. Snook calmly maintained his innocence. Full of disappointment, I realized that our time on Tosi Creek had come to an end.

The morning we left was chock-full of blue sky and bird song. Bill and I stood on the flagstones in front of Snook's porch to say good-bye. Despite the underlying anger, our parting was cordial, with Bill thanking Snook for allowing us

the privilege of sharing his pristine hideaway, and Snook
thanking us for all the work we had done to help him get
through the winter. Bill headed down the path, but I paused
long enough for Snook to reach out and grab my hand and
squeeze it tight. His hand felt like sun-warmed rough-out
leather with hundreds of horses running in the bulged veins.
He kissed my cheek and said, "Well, honey, I guess our play
house is all tore down. You take care of yourself." Snook didn't
need to confess his affection for me; his sad but twinkling blue
eyes revealed everything.

My heart split. I longed to stay with Snook and bask in the
warmth of his congenial nature. Then I remembered the vow
I had made to Bill on that winter night when he gave me the
ivory thunderbird. Snook owned his place, was married to
Evalyn, and had a host of friends and neighbors to look out for
him. Bill had no one but me. The weight of love and responsibility hung heavy around my neck. I turned and followed Bill
down the path.

Although we were of different generations, sexes, educations,
and cultural backgrounds and led different lifestyles, Snook
and I remained the best of friends. Our hearts twined, one and
the same. We both held dear the qualities of kindness and
compassion. I learned more about the way I was meant to live
my life in those eight months with Snook than I ever did in the
four years of college before or the long years of wilderness
living with Bill. I never received a paycheck from Snook or any
sort of in-kind exchange for the hours and days of labor I put
in on his ranch. What I did receive was the treasure of true
friendship, the invaluable gift of a very fine human being
passing on his knowledge and wisdom to another person.

∽

All the years I lived in Wyoming, I often went back to see
Snook. When I moved out of state, I wrote to him and he
responded, sending back notes that he had painfully scripted

with his arthritis-riddled hand to let me know he was doing all right in his high-country hideaway. One October when Evalyn was in California visiting her daughter, Snook died alone in his cabin, at the age of eighty. He had had a sore on his leg that would not heal. The wound broke open in the night, and Snook bled to death. When I received word of his passing, I felt a light go out in my life that would never be replaced. I knew of nothing else to do except have a wreath of evergreens and roses placed on his grave. I sent a hand-beaded buckskin medicine bag with a lock of my hair inside to a mutual friend and asked him to tie it up high in one of the pines that guarded Snook's cabin. On my walk that evening, I talked to Snook's spirit, trying to find a way to say thank you and good-bye.

The Flying A

Bill knew that I was not keen on the move away from the Moore Ranch. I said little, but I shied away from him at every opportunity. I thought of leaving, but I had no idea where I would go. The idea of going back to the Chicago area repelled me; the notion of trying to find a job in town made me feel sick to my stomach. Plus, despite all the difficulties we had weathered, I still loved him and hoped that somehow we would find a way to mend our fences and come out on the same side of things.

We settled in as caretakers in an old log palace on the Flying A Guest Ranch nestled between Big Twin Creek and Little Twin Creek above the Green River. Our job, simply, was to keep an eye on things for the absentee owner and prevent trespassers from causing damage. There were two ways into the Flying A: nine miles of dirt road and many gates across Jack Schwabacher's giant Quarter Circle 5 Ranch from the highway to Jackson Hole, or eight miles of worse dirt road and many gates through the O Bar Y Ranch from the highway to Pinedale.

Either way, Shangri-La wasn't easy to reach and would be snowed in during the winter.

Even though I had electric lights and hot running water for the first time, my silence turned sullen. I had been happy under Snook's fatherly wing of loving kindness. My heart had been broken many times before, but this time it felt shattered beyond repair. Bill tried to make it up to me by buying a couple of milk goats and picking up a German shepherd puppy he named Makwi. It was too late in the season to plant a garden, but he said we would buy peaches and apples to can. We had a freezer in which to keep fresh meat and vegetables from the store. He promised to take me on a pack trip into the high country and teach me to fly-fish. He did not sequester himself at night in a room alone. Instead he brought a single mattress into the master bedroom and set it up on the floor near the queen-size bed. I eyed the new sleeping situation with obvious distaste and stomped out. He came home one day with a black filly in the back of the truck and said, "Maybe if you behave yourself, she'll be yours by next spring."

I named the skittish unbroke filly Sis, and I often stole down to the corral to whisper secrets to her. Bit by bit she overcame her fear and came to snuffle my outstretched palm with her velvety nose. She wore a crooked white star between her deep, dark eyes. Her timid flightiness, the way she spooked back at any movement, reminded me of myself.

Late that summer, a couple rode in from Mexico on their way to Canada. They needed a place to rest their footsore horses and regroup before heading farther north. Len and Lisa had started out in Nevada, Missouri. They had learned a great deal about horses, gear, the backcountry, and the craziness of the modern world. They were determined, despite serious obstacles, to finish their quest. Bill and Len talked saddles and panniers and the best way to shoe their tender-hooved Fox Trotters. Because Bill had ridden from Canada to the Yellowstone in the early 1970s, he knew the country they might tra-

verse. Lisa and I holed up over cups of hot tea and commise-
rated about tough men, hard work, and long miles. Why did
we do it? What did we hope to gain in the end except for
weathered skin and no secure future? Laughing, I said, "I'd give
anything to have enough money for some decent panties." Lisa
pulled off her shirt, held up her dingy gray-white shabby bra,
and said, "Speaking of that, do you have a needle and thread?
This needs major repairs." Her beautiful suntanned breasts
looked like ripe melons.

Bill took to Lisa like a bee to a flower. He called her "the des-
ert rose" and catered to her whims. I didn't blame him; she
enchanted everyone. Young, lithe, fun, flirty, full of the devil,
and quick-witted, she engaged Bill in intellectual repartee and
made him roar with laughter. Once, after playing "Moonlight
Sonata" on the piano, Bill turned to her and said, "Do you play
an instrument?" Without pause, in a voice as smooth as good
whiskey, Lisa replied, "The only thing I know how to play is the
skin flute." To which Len replied, "She isn't kidding."

I left the trio joking by the fire and wandered down to the
corral to talk to Sis. I told her the truth. "This isn't anything
new. He's wanted other women before, and he's had them. It
doesn't even make me mad. It just makes me lonelier. Another
change is at hand. I wonder if we'll make it through the
winter."

When Len and Lisa saddled up a week later to continue their
adventure, I waved good-bye with regret. Despite twinges of
jealousy, I could tell that Lisa had been good for Bill. She had
brightened his spirits and given him reason to feel good about
himself. She was in awe of his wilderness skills and had honored him with compliments and praise. Snook, in his grand-
fatherly way, had done the same for me. What strange thing
happened to couples when they'd been together for some
years? What happened to the romance and passion and the
dreams that drifted apart like windblown clouds?

∾

Earlier that summer, when I was still living at the Moore
Ranch, Snook and Evalyn had invited me to join them at a
Fourth of July celebration on the Bar E Bar Ranch north of
Cora, Wyoming. I took rhubarb and walnut pies to the
gathering. Snook introduced me to a neighboring rancher in
his early fifties, Mick Buyer. Mick and his wife, Margie, ran a
couple hundred cows on their O Bar Y spread. Mick thought
that a gal who could still make a homemade pie might be
worth getting to know. That evening, when the time came for
me to leave, my old station wagon would not start. Mick
walked over, raised the hood, and cleaned the battery cables
with his pocketknife. The engine fired right up. I thought that a
man who could keep my car running might be a special friend.

∾

When Bill and I moved to the Flying A Ranch, we had to drive
through Mick's O Bar Y. It became a simple courtesy for us to
pick up his mail out at the highway and drop it off at his house.
Sometimes we stayed for a quick visit. Sometimes Mick's
home-for-the-summer wife, Margie, invited us to stay to
supper. Margie made a great sour cream chocolate cake, and
I coveted the recipe.

For twenty years, Mick and Margie had fought the four-to-
five-foot winter snows, raised Hereford cattle, and fed 450 head
of elk for the Wyoming Department of Game and Fish. Ranching was all Mick knew, and he told me he doubted he would
ever retire or do anything else but grow hay and feed cattle. A
half-dozen years earlier, with their two children, John and
Melody, grown, Margie had tired of deep snow, long winters,
hard work, and what she called "I think I'll go hang myself in
the barn loneliness." She purchased a small ranch in southern
Arizona where life was easier. She dreamed that Mick would
sell out in Wyoming and come south to retire. Mick was

doubtful about that. To him the notion seemed silly. How could he leave his land and his cattle?

Later that fall, when my path crossed Mick's again after Margie had left for Arizona, he was doing his feed chores with a team of mules that were as stubborn as he was, as unpredictable and intractable as the land he thrived on. I had begun to write for *Western Horseman* magazine, and the editor said their readers loved articles about mules. It took me several attempts to convince Mick to let me do an interview with him. Shy by nature, he wasn't sure he wanted to be in the limelight of a national magazine. Still, from the moment I met him, I knew that Mick Buyer was a man who never backed down from a challenge. Like Snook, Mick had been raised with horses. He had used two-, four-, and six-horse teams hooked to wagons, sleds, stone boats, mowers, rakes, and stackers. In the rough country of the O Bar Y, a team and a sled constituted the only way to feed stock during the snowbound winters. Like Snook, Mick welcomed the idea of having someone around to help with the chores and keep him company.

The O Bar Y

In the early winter of 1982, I began making the eight-mile round-trip trek on skis from the Flying A Ranch to work for Mick on the O Bar Y. Margie had hired me long-distance, saying, "It would sure help me not worry about Mick if he had someone to clean the house, do laundry, cook some meals, and help with the feeding. You keep track of your time, and I'll pay you in the spring." I was to work one day a week, at fifteen dollars a day.

Mick, meanwhile, was hobbling around. His horse had fallen while they were moving cattle, and as he said, he had "taken out a half-mile of sagebrush" with his right knee. He had a cantankerous old cowboy friend, Tom Astle, who came out to the ranch to help out when he had a mind to, but that wasn't often.

Bill was not pleased with my decision to be a "hired hand." His constant sarcasm and cold-shoulder silence drove me to spend more and more time with Mick, whose boyish warmth and flirty gentle teasing were a welcome respite. I couldn't wait to see Mick driving his team across the snow-covered horse pasture to the Haley meadow on his way to feed, his black Stetson snugged down, his face turned away from the hard wind, one hand holding the lines, the other raised in silent greeting as I skied past on my way to clean his house and make a hearty noon dinner.

My first cow-related job on the O Bar Y was feeding six bales of hay to twenty-two corralled heifer calves when Mick went to Arizona for Christmas with his family. I house-sat the Buyer home, fed the dogs and cats, made sure the pipes didn't freeze, and spent evenings shelling pecans as I watched the first TV I'd seen in my adult life. Mick's new satellite dish broadcast an endless array of movies, and I sat enraptured through *The French Lieutenant's Woman* and the Italian film *Wife Mistress*.

To use one of Mick's favorite expressions, I was dumber than a box of rocks and about as savvy as a fence post when it came to livestock. Still, I was eager to please and willing to learn. I didn't know that with every cow I fed or every new calf I handled, I was being initiated into a secret society that I would become committed to in a strangely loyal way. Was I once the girl who defended the right of wild horses to be on federal range, who fought stubbornly against anyone who wanted to shoot a coyote, who argued for wolf reintroduction, who was a confessed tree-hugger and protector of endangered species? Was I once the girl who believed that ranchers were rich, owned too much land, and prevented others from having some small piece of property for their own dream-come-true paradise? Had I really ever believed the old adage, which Bill espoused with vehemence, that the only thing dumber than a cow was a cowboy?

In my new role as an employee on the O Bar Y, I was easy to impress and indoctrinate into a whole new way of thinking about life on the land. I tried to capture the stark beauty and endearing hardships of Mick's daily life in photographs. For Christmas I gave him an album of pictures of him, his horses, his cattle, the snow-covered meadows, the ice-choked river, and the distant mountains. My dedication, written with a caring but very young hand, read: "To Mick, who loves the land most of all."

~

That winter, 1981–82, turned ferocious. As they had the year before at Snook's place, blizzards blew in constantly. I spent a lot of time shoveling the cabin roofs at the Flying A to keep them from collapsing. I worked overtime trying to keep my snowshoe/ski trail open to the O Bar Y. Lonely from too many winters on his own, Mick followed me from room to room as I cleaned the house, or stood leaning on the kitchen counter while I made rolls or attempted to concoct Margie's chocolate cake. I loved hearing stories about Mick growing up as a fifth-generation cowboy in Colorado, or his tales about being drafted into the army during the Korean War.

We grew addicted to each other's company. Smiling so much made my face ache. Laughing made my stomach hurt. I soaked up the attention Mick paid to me like a dried-up sponge. After a day at the O Bar Y, it was hard to ski home to the Flying A to find a cold kitchen, a sink full of dirty dishes, more laundry to be done, goats to milk, and supper to make. Bill had no desire to chat about my growing friendship with Mick. Neither did he want to hear glowing reports about my bovine education. As winter wore on, both of us received letters from Lisa. She and Len had made it to Canada and back to Missouri. They were in the midst of starting a company to design a new kind of saddle called Ortho-Flex.

On a gray day in February when I took a break from the domestic routine at the O Bar Y, Mick sat down across from me and said, "Laurie, I think I love you." It was a humble confession, fraught with fear and intense awkwardness. I knew it had taken a great deal of courage for a married man of Mick's generation to utter those words. It took even more courage for me to open my heart enough to hear them. I had lived with Bill for many years, and he had never used the word "love" with me. No man had ever told me he loved me. Pleased, but flustered, I stood up and backed away. I told Mick that I cared about him a great deal and that I liked working for him. I said, "I hope we can go on being good friends."

Had I forgotten what it was like to be loved? Surely my parents and sisters loved me. Snook had loved me. Some minuscule crack in my fragmented heart began to mend. I started to see the puzzle pieces of love, kindness, commitment, security, and a bright future fit together into a recognizable picture. Ever since leaving the Northfork, I had known that Bill and I were on borrowed time. Yet I still struggled with giving up on my original dream of coming west, living self-sufficiently and independent of society. I still carried the barely burning torch of a man, a woman, and paradise, and I continued to love Bill with a young girl's naïve ardor. How does a woman break an idealistic "first love is forever" promise? How could I know that it was possible to walk away from someone I loved?

∼

By the end of March, Mick was worn out from fighting the snow to feed the cattle. He was more than weary and ready to quit ranching. Margie told me by telephone, "I've been telling him this for years. Why won't he listen to me?" The answer, which I could not verbalize at the time, was that he loved the O Bar Y too much to consider leaving.

By the time calving time came in April, Mick was on one leg from a knee operation. He managed to cripple around through the snow by putting bails on the bottom of his crutches. I learned how to harness the team of Clydes and feed off bales to the snowbound cows, bulls, and horses. It was a bad spring, wet and cold. The calves from the first-calf heifers scoured and died. We dragged them off for the coyotes and poked pills down the cold, raw throats of the ones left alive. I

nursed a paralyzed calf for days, massaging its useless legs,
coaxing it to stand, which it could not do. Its ma was gentle
and wise. She stood over her calf so it could rise up on its front
knees and suck. But it would never be well, and the sight of it
lying wet and dirty in its own excrement sickened me.

One morning while Mick held the horses' lines with one
hand and his crutches in the other, I slid off the sled and
walked into the barn alone. It was dimly lit by early sun, the
silence like a cathedral. I sorted off the cow, used a sledge-
hammer to stun the crippled calf, and cut its throat. When I
stepped outside to wipe the antler-handled knife Bill had made
for me in the pristine snow, I said, "I'll drag it off later."
Looking up, I saw Mick's home-from-college son John staring
at me. His eyes called me cruel. I wanted to tell him that the
line between cruelty and kindness was fine, so very, very fine.

When branding time came, the corrals were dry, and a thick
haze hung in the air full of hot-iron smoke and dust from four
hundred frantic hooves tromping the ground. Mick's knee gave
out, and he couldn't kneel to castrate the bull calves. I had been
one half of a two-man wrestling team tasked with holding the
calves on the ground, but I turned my job over to another, took
Mick's knife and emasculator, and went to work. As she turned
her head away from the knife, Mick's daughter, Melody,
grimaced and laughed. She began to call me Miss Blood and
Guts. I didn't mind. Her joking made me smile. At last I had
grown tough enough to do a man's job in a man's world and be
paid for my effort.

I doubt that Bill ever understood the relative peace and
sense of belonging that I found with Mick and his family on
the O Bar Y. I had come into an acceptance of my own abilities.
I knew what kind of life I wanted and needed to sustain me. I
also had finally figured out that my desperate heart had to have
constant nurturing and encouragement to be happy. Bill
remained scornful and could not believe that I would throw
away a life "wild and free" for an existence of constant

servitude. With my first paycheck, I bought a package of colored cotton panties and a kerosene lamp for the small cabin on the O Bar Y that Margie and Mick had offered to me if I would come to work for them full-time at three hundred dollars a month plus room and board.

Bill drove off in miffed silence, bound for Nevada, Missouri, to see Len and Lisa. I stayed at the Flying A to take care of the goats and dogs and horses. I spent many hours down at the corral with Sis, now halter-broke but still spooky. The filly's dark eyes asked me not to leave her there alone.

When Bill returned, I tried to talk to him. I wanted him to know that I had to leave to save myself, but that I hoped we could be friends. He could not comprehend the possibility. A friend was someone who stayed and stuck it out. If I left, I became the enemy. I touched the ivory thunderbird around my neck and asked, "May I keep this?" He said, "No," and reached for my throat. I stepped back and slipped the leather thong over my head. He snatched the thunderbird from my hand as if I had stolen the carving from him.

As I gathered books and clothes, he stood stoic and silent in the doorway watching me, his arms crossed, his face blank, his eyes flint-hard and fathomless. I didn't have much to pack. I simply took all that I had learned from him and left the rest behind. In the end, Bill was kind. He let me go.

The hardest thing for me as I left for the O Bar Y was telling the dogs to stay, hearing the goats bleating in the pasture, and seeing Sis, her fine head hung over the gate, watching me drive away through the rain.

Epilogue

I worked for Mick and Margie Buyer on the O Bar Y from 1983 to 1988. When Margie returned from Arizona for the summers, she and I managed the household together. Both of us worked in the hayfields and helped with the cattle. Mick and I became the talk of the valley when our friendship turned into a love affair. Mick and Margie divorced after years of separation and sold the O Bar Y. Margie returned to her ranch in Arizona. Mick bought land on the South Fork of the South Platte River near Fairplay, Colorado, where we built a log cabin and started another herd of cattle. We married in July of 1989.

Tears still needle my eyes when I remember the seasons I lived on the banks of wild rivers in Montana and Wyoming. It was not easy to give up on my dream, especially one that I sacrificed so much of myself to try and obtain. I thought for a long time that Bill and I would someday understand each other. I hoped that we would sit down together to talk about the things that had happened to us. I held on to that naïve illusion for twenty-five more years before I finally let go.

On and off, Bill wrote to me. Although his vitriolic attacks on my character obscured any opportunity for forgiveness or friendship, his accounts of life as a "dweller of the silences" still had the power to enchant. After roaming for years, often living in a tepee camp with his dogs and horses, he finally settled down. With his mother's assistance he bought a small acreage, horse-logged out some large pines, and hand-built a new Val Halla overlooking another remote river. As far as I know, he never invited another woman to share his rarefied existence. Instead, he contented himself with the companionship of a pack of hybrid wolves, his horses, and the company of occasional special visitors. He still hunts, tans buckskin, grows most of his own food, makes his own clothing, forges knives, and engraves stunning animal portraits on antler rosettes. He does well in guarding his hard-won privacy and his singular aloneness.

Acknowledgments

Many thanks to early readers for their close scrutiny and sound advice: Kathlene Sutton, Natalia Brothers, and my mother, Joan Wagner. Special appreciation to Matt Bokovoy and Charles Rankin at the University of Oklahoma Press for their visionary editing and unending patience in bringing this story into the light. Warm embraces to W. C. Jameson, Dale Walker, Richard Wheeler, Max Evans, Nat Sobel, Candy Moulton, and Nancy Curtis for their encouragement and for believing in this book. And for Bill, "Makwi Witco," without whom I would never have come west.

∽

Some of these essays appeared in earlier versions in *Leaning into the Wind: Women Write from the Heart of the West* and *Woven on the Wind: Women Write about Friendship in the Sagebrush West* (Houghton-Mifflin), *Hot Coffee, Cold Truth: Living and Writing the West* (University of New Mexico Press), the *Backwoodsman,* the *Fence Post,* the *Kalispell Livestock Weekly News, Roundup Magazine,* the *SAC,* and *Western Horseman.* I extend my thanks to the original publishers.